The University of Michigan
MBA/MA in Asian Studies
Retrospection and Reflections

This book was compiled and edited by Linda Lim, Professor Emerita at the University of Michigan, from 2015-2019, with assistance from Neal X. McKenna of the Lieberthal-Rogel Center for Chinese Studies.

THE UNIVERSITY OF MICHIGAN MBA/MA IN ASIAN STUDIES

RETROSPECTION AND REFLECTIONS

A Bicentennial Contribution

LINDA LIM

Published in the United States of America by Michigan Publishing
Services

DOI: http://doi.org/10.3998/mpub.11604093

ISBN 978-1-60785-505-7 (paper)
ISBN 978-1-60785-506-4 (e-book)
ISBN 978-1-60785-602-3 (open-access)

An imprint of Michigan Publishing Services, Maize Books serves
the publishing needs of the University of Michigan community by
making high-quality scholarship widely available in print and
online. It represents a new model for authors seeking to share
their work within and beyond the academy, offering streamlined
selection, production, and distribution processes. Maize Books is
intended as a complement to more formal modes of publication
in a wide range of disciplinary areas.

http://www.maizebooks.org

CONTENTS

CHAPTER 1.

ACKNOWLEDGMENTS

This history of the University of Michigan's MBA/MA in Asian Studies dual degree program, and its graduates, was conceived as a contribution to the celebration of U-M's bicentennial (1817–2017) given the university's long engagement with Asia and continued scholarly distinction in Asian studies.

Thanks are due to the university's Center for Japanese Studies, Lieberthal-Rogel Center for Chinese Studies, Center for Southeast Asian Studies, Center for South Asian Studies, and Stephen M. Ross School of Business for their collaborative initiation and support of this interdisciplinary program over more than a quarter-century and for their financial support. Gary D. Krenz, Executive Director of the U-M Bicentennial Office, kindly allowed this volume to be included as a bicentennial publication.

Above all, thanks are due to the alumni of the program for contributing their biographies, reflections, and photographs and to Neal X. McKenna of the Lieberthal-Rogel Center for bringing the volume to publication.

Linda Y.C. Lim
Professor Emerita of Corporate Strategy and International Business
Faculty Associate, CJS, LRCCS, CSEAS
November 2017

CHAPTER 2.

PROGRAM HISTORY AND FACULTY REFLECTIONS

LINDA LIM

HISTORY

The joint MBA/MA in Asian Studies degree program at the University of Michigan was begun around 1980 by John Campbell and Robert Cole, professors of political science and sociology of Japan, respectively. Campbell became Director of the Center for Japanese Studies (CJS) in 1982, and the program's first graduate, David Quigley, graduated in 1983. Once the program was established in the Rackham Graduate School, the other U.S. Department of Education (US/ED) Title VIA National Resource Centers (NRCs) on Asia and other world areas could use it to build their MA programs. Later the Michigan Business School—probably Vern Terpstra, Chair of the International Business department, and later Ed Miller, Associate Dean for International Business—collaborated with John and the Asia centers.

Campbell also started the East Asia Business Program (EABP at CJS and Center for Chinese Studies or CCS) when US/ED came out with its Title VIB Business and International Education competitive grant program, while Pete Gosling, professor of geography and anthropology, obtained the same grant for the Southeast Asia Business Program (SEABP at then Center for

Southeast Asian Studies or CSEAS) in 1984. We were in Lane Hall with all the area studies centers—SEABP on the second floor and EABP in the basement, where the Association of Asian Studies (AAS) also had its offices. The Asian language programs were in the Frieze Building (now replaced by the North Quad complex), diagonally across State Street from Lane Hall, while CCS had faculty offices in the Corner House (now replaced by 300 N. Thayer where the Department of Asian Languages and Cultures or ALC—formerly Far Eastern Languages and Literatures—is located).

Campbell later obtained Federal funding for the Japan Technology Management Program (JTMP). Between this program and Foreign Language and Area Studies (FLAS) Fellowship support from the Title VIA Centers, we managed to provide fellowships and summer internships for some of the students in the MBA/MA in Asian Studies program, while others earned hourly wages in various capacities as student assistants. EABP and SEABP ran business conferences and executive education seminars (like Negotiating with the Japanese and Emerging Asian Economies), while SEABP also ran a biennial faculty research conference and started a library and a newsletter, which later evolved into the peer-reviewed *Journal of Asian Business* covering the whole region. Kenneth DeWoskin, professor of ancient Chinese history in ALC, was instrumental in establishing EABP's executive seminars. Clyde Stoltenberg and Heidi Tietjen were hired to run the EABP while a succession of MA and MBA graduates (Greg Kesten, Nidhi Gangwar), students, and staff (Helen White, Sandy Reoma) worked for SEABP until Jason Eyster was hired to run that program and edit the *Journal of Asian Business* (which closed in 2015 after a 25-year run).

JTMP also brought some productive collaboration among the business and engineering schools as well as CJS, producing a book by John Campbell, John Ettlie, and Jeffrey Liker, *Engineered in Japan: Japanese Technology-Management Practices* (New

York: Oxford University Press, 1995), which won the 1996 Shingo Manufacturing Research Prize.

In the 1980s, Japan was booming and emerging as a fierce competitor for U.S. business, especially Michigan's auto industry, so there was great interest in learning about Japanese business and society. The International Business department offered as many as three sections of over 60 students each on the Japanese Business System well into the 1990s, when we had three Japanese-literate faculty members in the Michigan Business School—Mary Yoko Brannen, David Methe, and Tom Roehl—later followed by a fourth, David Weinstein. China's "opening" beginning in the 1980s and the 1990s boom in Southeast Asia also attracted students.

In 1989, I wrote the grant proposal that won the business school the first Title VI Center for International Business Education (CIBE), for which I served as Interim Director until Brad Farnsworth was hired from the Yale-in-China program in 1991 to run it. SEABP later folded into CIBE, and EABP was terminated, leaving CIBE to be the main unit coordinating the joint degree program with CJS, CCS, and CSEAS. CIBE closed in 2014 after Brad Farnsworth's departure, having already refocused its activities on undergraduate study abroad, now under Ross Global Initiatives.

CURRENT STATUS

As our list of alumni shows, the MBA/MA in Asian Studies program eventually ended in the late 2000s for the following reasons, many if not most of them common to other "top 10" MBA programs.

- The MBA program shifted to higher enrollment of older students, with average 700 plus GMAT scores and five years' work experience, putting them past the ideal age for learning a difficult new language.

- Higher MBA and MA tuition increased the opportunity

cost of an extra year of school and the competition for FLAS awards from the area centers. Other Ross dual degree programs have flourished because of endowed fellowship and internship support, while most Asia MA dual degrees are with other professional schools, mainly Law, Public Policy, Social Work, and Natural Resources and Environment.

- CJS and CCS MA programs required ever-higher levels of prior language learning (a minimum of three completed years) for admission and a faculty generally oriented more toward the humanities than the professions.

- MBA job placement skewed sharply away from general management and operational industry positions, which are intrinsically "global," toward consulting, finance, and marketing (in that order), which tend to be more domestic especially for entry-level MBA positions.

- The introduction of off-campus Multidisciplinary Action Projects (MAP) in the second half (winter semester) of MBA1 and other features of the core curriculum made it impossible for MBA students to take a full academic year of language.

- MBAs now focus on remunerative stateside summer internships that have become a major entry to post-graduation jobs as well as a means to recoup some of their high tuition costs, limiting their interest in less remunerative international internships and summer language learning.

- MBA (and BBA) programs have shifted toward "study abroad lite," including international MAP, global project courses, exchange programs, and student-organized M-Treks, none of which require language or country knowledge or help track students into international careers (i.e., the location of projects is immaterial to students' subsequent careers).

- The number of international students from Asia (nearly one-third of the full-time MBA program, mainly from China and India) has greatly increased, coupled with employers' preference for hiring Asian nationals for in-country and Asia-related U.S. jobs rather than Americans and expatriates.

- In the early 2000s, the Deans' office dismantled the over 40-year-old International Business department, leaving the field without an institutional home, support, and advocacy for the MBA/MA in Asian Studies program and for Asia expert faculty, who are no longer hired for their Asia expertise.

- Japan's "two lost decades" and the Asian financial crisis of 1997–1998 and its aftermath created the impression that business opportunities in the region had declined.

Interestingly, the most lasting legacy of the MBA/MA program may be the Asia Business Conference (ABC), which was started in 1989 as Japan Day with Adam Orlan, Jim Roche, Paul Martin, and LeAnn Eriksson, and possibly also LeRoy Howard, Jeff Protzel, and Michelle Gross. Joe Osha and Dave Most got involved in 1990. In 1991, when LeAnn was President of the International Business Club, she brought in Durk Jaeger, CEO of P&G, as keynote speaker, and the conference subsequently expanded to include more of Asia, with Andrew Masterman, Amy Rubin, Pat Friel, Cynthia Tragge, Rajeev Lakra, and Charles Breer (who for many years secured Northwest Airlines as a corporate sponsor) participating.

Now covering all of Asia, the conference remains the longest-running such event at a U.S. business school. The "follower" conferences have morphed, for example, Harvard's Asia Business Conference (since 1994) into a combined conference with its

Law School and other units, Northwestern's Kellogg School of Management's into a Greater China and an Emerging Markets Conference joint with the Chicago Council on Global Affairs (last offered in 2016), Wharton's and Berkeley's both intermittent and downsized with only a handful of speakers each.

Our ABC survives (so far!) for four main reasons: (a) consistent financial support from the Asia area centers; (b) Asia's continued rise in the business world; (c) ABC's evolution into a student club heavily populated and led by Asian nationals and Asian Americans (MBAs, BBAs and others), whose numbers in the student body have greatly increased; and (d) consistent support from faculty, including the now many Asian-national Ross faculty who are available and willing to serve as faculty moderators for conference panels (reportedly a constraint at some of our peer schools).

But this conference also faces challenges. The main reason is the continued "balkanization" of the student body, at Ross and elsewhere in the university, into "identity groups." The Indian Subcontinent Business Association started intermittently offering an India Business Conference, which finally became institutionalized as an annual event (its eighth iteration occurring in 2017) with business school funding and staff support for an India Initiative. Various China conferences were started, with the current survivors being the China Entrepreneurs' Network, which changes its form every year (most recently an activity of Chinese and Chinese-American undergraduates), an annual China Auto Conference organized by the U-M Transportation Research Institute, and the annual event of the LS&A undergraduate Association for Chinese Economic Development, all of which have been running for about six to eight years each. Law School students—who used to participate in the ABC—also ran an annual Asian Law Conference (which started as a China Law Conference) for a number of years.

The problems that this proliferation of Asia events present, not just for ABC, include (a) competition for speakers (there are only so many willing to travel on their own dollar to Ann Arbor to speak to students); (b) competition for sponsorship funds from on-campus units including student government and the Asia area centers; (c) competition for student attention or "mindshare" (e.g., the real risk of "China fatigue"); and (d) most seriously, competition for space, both available dates on the school calendar and for conference and hotel rooms during the academic year.

Those of you who attended the 2010 and 2015 ABCs and MBA/MA reunions noted that there were virtually no "white people" in the audience. Usually there are more "white Americans" on a panel than in the audience, on which some invited panel speakers have also commented. One asked me, "Aren't Americans interested in Asia anymore?" I explained that some (not many) in the audience are Asian Americans, but that still begged his (implied) query as to why white Americans aren't interested. We actually do have "regular MBAs" (including whites) who studied Japanese, (more usually) Chinese, or (less usually) Korean as undergrads; are fluent in the languages; and even worked for several years in these countries (usually China, including in provincial cities and as entrepreneurs). But (a) they don't feel the need to learn more about Asia formally, and (b) are often taking the MBA to "reintegrate" themselves into the United States and particularly to enter the U.S. business world.

The 27th annual conference took place in January 2018 with a full slate of panels and speakers, despite difficulties raising sponsorship funds. It is now an all-undergrad event led by BBAs, with the organizing team of over 50 students being nearly all Asian nationals or Asian Americans, for whom it is the largest club event.

MY THOUGHTS ON ALL THIS

One of the privileges of being a faculty member at a university such as Michigan is that "you get to see the future before it arrives," since we are educating and training young "talent" from all nations who will be the business, professional, and societal leaders of the future. While this is good, and I greatly appreciate my ever-expanding network of Asian-national former students and other U-M alumni in Asia, there are also dangers and disappointments resulting from the balkanization that I referred to above. Mainly, and perhaps paradoxically, the more globally integrated our world becomes, the less we pay attention to the diversity among us and the more divided and insular we become in our personal and social as well as professional interactions. What we do becomes defined by who we are rather than what we know—or, everything becomes a form of "identity politics," and not just on campus.

At U-M, once and still a bastion of "area and language studies," all area studies, including the strongest, Asian studies, are constantly beleaguered in a higher education world that increasingly questions the "usefulness" (typically measured by salary in first post-graduation job) of any kind of education worth paying for, privately or publicly. Learning about others, including their languages and cultures, falls into the "not useful" category, whereas learning about ourselves is good "diversity." Thus most of our language courses and nearly all Less Commonly Taught Languages (LCTLs) are filled with "heritage students": for example, Indian Americans in Hindi, Korean Americans in Korean, Filipino-Americans in Filipino, Vietnamese Americans in Vietnamese, and so on. Chinese is a partial exception due to its assumed commercial allure, and there are few Japanese Americans to take Japanese. The LCTLs perennially at risk of being discontinued due to low enrollments are those whose native speakers do not immigrate to the United States but rather return home, to Indonesia and Thailand (the world's fourth and 21st most populous countries, respectively), so there are no heritage students.

With the Trump Administration proposing to eliminate the US/ED Title VI program that has funded U-M's NRCs and FLAS Fellowships on Asia and other regions for over a half-century, as well as the Fulbright-Hays and other international studies programs, the retrenchment from area studies and non-heritage foreign language learning at U.S. universities is likely to continue. Chinese and Japanese language are among the exceptions at the undergraduate level, the latter reportedly in part because of the popularity of anime.

At Ross, student clubs and activities are increasingly populated exclusively by nationals. The Greater China Business Association's members are all from the People's Republic only (though it was founded by Hong Kong and Taiwan students in the early 2000s), and very few if any non-Chinese attend their annual Chinese New Year celebration in the school. Similarly, one year the Japanese Business Association had a Japan Culture Night that was attended mostly by Japanese, the India Business Conference is attended mostly by Indians, and the Korean Business Association was once heavily divided on whether to include Korean Americans who do not speak Korean. An Asian Business Association that existed for a while in the 2000s became defunct as a result, and an ASEAN Business Association that formed in 2012 "because everyone else has their own club" has few, mainly social, activities. I have served as nominal faculty adviser for any number of Asian American clubs that sputter for a year or two and then disappear. Most of these ethno-national groups are "career networking" organizations and pressure groups for admissions and job placement in the United States and are not focused on learning about business in Asia.

In some sense Asia, especially Asian business, has become both mainstreamed (so no one feels the need to learn about it separately in any depth) and ghettoized (so that only those from the culture are interested and "allowed" to express and celebrate it). Diversity has come to mean every ethno-national group having its own club and its own event. An effort in 2013 to reconstitute an International Business Club (killed long ago by all this separatism) populated mainly by the self-defined "left-outs"—that is, few Latin Americans, Europeans, Middle

Easterners, and Africans, with a sprinkling of Asians and no Americans—failed when the business school advised against their holding a planned one-day conference I was helping with because it would coincide with St. Patrick's Day weekend! This is similar to ABC and the now-annual all-American MBA Ski Weekend competing yearly for an early February date. Americans still control and dominate the "sections" into which MBA students are divided, the "section culture," and functional clubs (finance, women, etc.). Students themselves note that in the Winter Garden (the atrium lobby which is the "hub" of the Ross building), "everyone is in their own group." The crowd looks diverse, but everyone is clustered—not by ethnicity necessarily but by nationality and language.

My Business in Asia class also looks very different than when our MBA/MAs took it—or took Japanese Business System or Business in China, all subsequently collapsed into my all-Asia course, which has ceased with my retirement. Now white Americans are a visible minority, with most of the students being Asian nationals or Asian Americans. It's great for learning and sharing among Asians, but the vast majority of Americans and non-Asians in the school do not participate, ironically at a time when Asia has become ever more important as a market, competitor, partner, and employer. Years ago, someone told me that American students didn't want to take this class because they would be forced to listen to the strange accents and imperfect English of foreign Asians and felt uncomfortable "being in the minority." Interestingly, the white-mostly-men in the evening MBA program don't seem to have such hang-ups, perhaps because they are more likely to have worked in Asia and with Asians (e.g., through the globalized auto industry and its suppliers).

There is great interest in travel—hence the popularity of international MAP and other "global project" courses. The main activity of the Japan Business Association appears to be organizing an annual Japan Trek, essentially a tourism activity for American MBAs, similar to India Trek, Vietnam Trek, and others that provide 10-day-holiday-bus-tours-with-my-friends for 40–70 MBAs each, in which the only non-American participants are a couple of the foreign-country nationals who assume responsibility for arranging the tour. "Treks" are a bonding experience for Americans, not a learning experience for all, and students who go on them do not participate in ABC or enroll in my Business in Asia class because they are really not that interested in Asia or Asians.

OUR MBA/MA GRADUATES

You can see now why I am so nostalgic for the heyday of our MBA/MA in Asian Studies program, which correlated closely with the first 20 years of my career at Michigan. The students in the program were different from the mainstream then and now. They chose to be different, were not afraid to be a "minority" and to operate outside their "comfort zone," and recognized the value of and were willing to learn the foreign language that would help them to survive, learn, and enjoy being in Asia. They were motivated by adventure and excitement rather than by money, and they had enthusiasm, daring, and entrepreneurial initiative (as in starting the ABC and running the IBC). They got used to and even appreciated being "outsiders" in both the business school world (whose corporate values and narrow interests they often did not share) and the Asian studies world (where they were marginalized and even discriminated against for being business students rather than "pure" humanities scholars of Asia).

The "career panel" that some of you spoke at in 2015 prompted this question from an Asian undergrad, "Why did you do something so hard (working as a foreigner in Asia 30 years ago), instead of choosing something easier?" and LeAnn's immediate and memorable response, "What's fun about easy?" For through it all, the MBA/MAs had fun and were funny, providing for me a rare comfortable spot in a dual institutional environment (the business school and Asian Studies) where I too was an outsider.

In that duality, and comfort with it, lies, I believe, the advantage many of you have experienced in your lives as well as your careers. Some of you have continued to "follow the different path" and found contentment there, in art, music, healthcare, social work. Others continue to "scale the corporate heights," in some cases leapfrogging over or outcompeting MBAs who took more conventional paths. For some of you, Asia came before the program, for others right after, and for yet others, it never came or has waned as a factor in your careers, lives, and interests. Many of those who worked in Asia have crossed the geographical/cultural boundaries of China, Japan, and Southeast Asia, in both your friendships and professional careers. China specialists are as likely to work in Southeast Asia and vice versa, and Japan specialists work in both China and Southeast Asia, as well as Korea. This of course reflects the "real world" of international business these days, including regional rather than single-country supply chains and market orientations as well as expatriate placements where functional expertise, seniority, and short tenures (see, e.g., Mike Little's essay in this volume) trump any perceived need to "see the world through the eyes of the other," which language learning, deep knowledge, and understanding provide that Google Translate and short travel courses cannot.

I hope you think that the extra year was beneficial at least as a short-term consumption good, if not a long-term investment in learning how to look at a differentiated world with different eyes. I love the diversity in the paths you have chosen. Most of all, I wish we still had students, graduates, and a world like you.

CHAPTER 3.

ALUMNI REFLECTIONS

Arranged chronologically by graduation date

STEVE DEAN—CSEAS 1987

As I read Linda's invite to write a few words about my experience with the Center for Southeast Asian Studies, my wife and I are having breakfast at Warung Liku Nakula, on the outskirts of Denpasar, Bali, celebrating our 25th wedding anniversary and eating $1 Ayam Betutu. The warung is simple, with no discernible door separating the interior from a few tables outside and the traffic beyond. The food: chicken mixed rice with local spices. Absolutely delicious!

Most doorways we walk through barely get a notice. Some change our lives forever.

I remember walking through the doorway into Linda Lim's office on a pleasant fall afternoon during my first semester in B-school. Papers and books everywhere.

Me: "Hi, I'm interested to find out about the joint MBA/MA program. Can you tell me about it?"

Linda: "Sure, but let me ask first, would you be interested in a scholarship?"

Me: "Yes, sure!"

Linda: "Write me an essay...."

Topic: "Why I want an FLAS scholarship and what I will do

with it." Okay, let's see: Can I say that I want the scholarship so that I can graduate without debt? Maybe not. Let's go with this: "I will use the FLAS to pursue my interest in international business and to help American companies build their businesses in the fastest growing sub-region in the world. I have lived in Honduras, have tutored Cambodian war refugee kids for three years during college, and am keen to empower my capability to build a career in Southeast Asia. ..." Yup, that sounds good. Pure fiction, of course. (Do I really see myself having a career in Asia?)

Based on the power of this prose, or perhaps due to a lack of competition, I receive the scholarship, laugh in delight through every lecture that Pete Gosling delivers, and without Rick Smith's "I'm going regardless" chutzpah, join the line of would-be interns and MBA recruits vying for a position with the few international companies that recruit at Michigan at the time. None see the diamond-in-the-rough in front of them, and I join NBD Bancorp on Woodward Avenue in Detroit upon graduation.

The bank is the most international firm of the many that gave me job offers (two) and promises a fast track to working internationally: put in 10 good years, and if you play your cards right, you can go to, um, Germany. Hmmm.

Eighteen months after graduation, Linda calls and asks if I know anyone who would be interested in a marketing job with Gerber baby products in Singapore. "Linda, please put in my name." "Ah, Steve, you're a finance guy." "Yes, please put my name in anyway."

I go through the interview process, and Gerber tells me that they like me very much, well enough to rank me #2 among the job candidates ... but alas, there is only one position, and they have selected an internal candidate who has been with the company for five years, comes from the marketing department, etc. ("You're a finance guy, Steve") ... "Of course, we will call you if anything changes." "Sure, thanks very much."

This is the last week of May 1989. Less than a week later, on

June 4, 1989, the tanks roll through Tiananmen Square, and the internal marketer says "Beijing-Singapore? Same-Same. I don't want to go to Asia." A tragedy that echoes still, a silver lining for me. Gerber calls back, and 10 months later, I land in Singapore.

Roll the tape back to grad school days: some of the finest evenings I spend in grad school are on Saturday nights at Linda and Pete's home with people from the center and with those somehow connected to Southeast Asia. The food is delicious, the conversation lively. One of the people I meet is a young grad student from Singapore doing a PhD in Sociology, Phyllisis Ngin (the original Dr. Phyl, now married to MBA/MA Drew Kraisinger). When Phyllisis finds out that I am moving to Singapore, she gives me a list of her friends to look up and unbeknownst to me writes glowing letters of introduction to some on the list ("for an *ang-moh*, he is not bad..."). The recipient of one of these letters is a lovely teacher named June, who is now my wife, and mother to our one son, Brendan.

Once Brendan is born, as Gerber is taken over, and as its Asian HQ moves from Singapore to Manila, I decide to get back into the financial world and give up traveling three weeks a month to be able to see Brendan grow up. As my master's essay was on the Stock Exchange of Singapore, I decide to go into stock broking ... and end up two years on with a front-row seat to the Asian financial crisis, which I must say is viscerally far more of an education in terms of how Mr. Market works than was my previous research. A privilege of being one of the few Americans on the trading floor of G.K. Goh during the crisis is getting the occasional visit from G.K. himself during lunch time. G.K. is a self-made billionaire (when Singapore still occasionally produced these) and has one piece of insight that sticks with me still ("Yeah, Asia looks bad now, but you Americans are the ones who are going to really screw it up").

Since joining Thomson Reuters 10 years ago, I have become an "arms dealer," selling the weapon of choice in the new business wars: data. Are you an asset manager who wants to federate all of that internal data (mall foot-traffic data with expected dividends and all of the private data you have been collecting over the years), meta-tag it, and stitch it together into a knowledge graph? I have a solution for you. Are you a regulator who wants a master key to understand which foreign counter-parties have just pounded your currency? I have a data feed that should do the trick.

As we leave Warung Liku Nakula, the driver of the taxi that we flag down is chatty. The busy season is just starting, and it is a bit rainy, but it is lovely to sit inside listening to the rain in the evening. His children have grown and started to work. Both live in Bali. Having never really needed to use my Indonesian for my day-to-day work, I am pleasantly surprised to be able to fill the 20-minute ride with him, using my very rusty Bahasa. I hope this will improve now that I have relocated to Jakarta with Thomson Reuters.

Walking through some doorways changes our lives forever. Whether it be work, wife, or life, walking through the doorway that fair fall day in Ann Arbor to speak to Linda has, indeed, changed my life in so many ways, and in ways for which I will always be grateful. Thank you, Linda, CSEAS, and the University of Michigan. Go Blue!

WM PATRICK CRANLEY—CCS 1988

Born and bred in Baltimore, Maryland, I first became interested in China while an undergraduate studying International Relations at Brown University. I "entered" the subject via philosophy and religion and "settled" into the politics and economics of the People's Republic. After two years working in Washington, DC, I decided to pursue a business degree and combine it with Chinese studies. "Way back then" (in the mid-1980s), there were only a few such programs in the United States, and the University of Michigan had assembled a China Studies "dream team" in the form of Professors Michel Oksenberg, Robert Dernberger, Kenneth Lieberthal, Albert

Feuerwerker, Rhoads Murphey, Ken DeWoskin, and others. Professors Linda Lim, Vern Terpstra, and Gunter Dufey were over at the B-school promoting global business studies, then an area of studies in its infancy.

I think, as with most joint degree students, my academic experience was a bit schizophrenic, bouncing between the money-focused business school and the often-esoteric atmosphere at Corner House. Both programs were stimulating, both were challenging, and both provided top-notch intellectual mentors. My experience was further fragmented by spending a year at the Hopkins-Nanjing Center, which added valuable on-the-ground experience to my studies in Ann Arbor. I also spent one glorious summer in Ann Arbor studying intensive third-year Chinese.

My thesis was on the nascent securities markets in China, and through the interviewing program at the business school, I received job offers in banking, real estate, and insurance. I signed on with CIGNA International Reinsurance and ended up in Singapore, its regional headquarters for Asia, within a year. Some six years after that, I moved to China with my wife and two children—and we've been there ever since. So it's easy for me to state that the U-M MBA/MA program was absolutely essential to realizing my goal of a career in Chinese business. Sincere thanks to the Blue & Gold!

MIKE DUNNE—CCS/CSEAS 1990

Oh, if only we could tap a pause button and capture moments forever. A camera comes close. So do voice recordings. The motion picture nearly gets us there.

Is there anything more precious than moments in time?

I remember like it was yesterday one afternoon in Pete Gosling's class and our surprisingly entrancing discussions of rice and its importance to Southeast Asian culture.

Pete encouraged us to go see for ourselves how rice featured in just about every meal and how meals were the cornerstone of life in that large swathe of humanity that stretched from Chiang Mai to Semarang and all points in between.

Pete did offer one important heads-up. Beware of those idyllic photos of people working in the rice fields of luxuriant green as far as the eye can see. Actually, he informed us from direct experience, the work of planting and harvesting rice is a real backbreaker. Don't go there, he warned.

In the comfort of our Ann Arbor classroom, I was doubtful. How exciting it would be to get calf-deep in some expansive Thai Isaan rice paddies? Splash around a bit. Soak in the sun's rays.

When after arriving in Thailand and making it my home I suggested an afternoon of rice planting to Thai friends from Khon Kaen, they look horrified, winced, and cried: Planting rice? "Ooooohweee dai laew. Raaaaauuan maaaak!" Translation: Hotter than hell out there. No way!

Professor Gosling knows his stuff.

If Pete offered deep wisdom and gave us the freedom to discover things for ourselves, Professor Linda Lim was the candid and persistent drill instructor, training undisciplined Americans like me to wake up and pay attention.

Linda was the first to open my eyes to the fact that there was so much more to Asia than China. She encouraged me to study Thai and to explore Southeast Asia.

Little did I know that she also already had a grand plan for me.

When many years later my wife, Merlien (native of Jakarta), and I paid our first visit to Linda and Pete in their home, Linda took me aside and offered a kind of Linda-esque compliment.

"Mike, I'm so happy that you've married an Indonesian and not a Chinese woman," she said.

Taken aback, I managed to say only, "Oh, yeah? How come?"

"Well, if you had married a Chinese, you would know on day two of the marriage that she was totally in charge. But with an Indonesian girl, well, she is also totally in charge. But the approach is much more subtle, so you won't realize it until three or four years from now."

And then she topped off her observation with the trademark Linda Lim laughter. The kind of knowing chuckle that reminded me of days in the classroom when her smile would be a way of signaling just how much I still needed to learn.

Robert Frost captured my imagination when he wrote about a road less traveled. It is thanks to Pete and Linda that I've had the opportunity to take those roads, living and working in Indonesia, Thailand, and China—the most fascinating places on planet Earth in our lifetime.

I've ridden elephants in Chiang Rai; walked the sandy coastline of Vietnam; driven the chaotic roads across Java; hiked Borobudur; taken the train from top to toe in Malaysia; basked in the magic art of Ubud, Bali; played countless days of softball in Manila and Singapore; enjoyed supremely delicious seafood in Hua Hin; and yes, listened until dawn to the Thai folk singers in Surin, JW Black and soda and a big bucket of ice on the side.

What precious memories. Thank you, Pete and Linda.

PATRICK FRIEL—CSEAS 1991

I grew up in a small town in northeast Ohio. When I was in high school, the Iranian Revolution erupted and piqued my interest in the Middle East. I was convinced the United States was ill equipped to interact with the region, so I completed a BA in Middle Eastern Studies at The Ohio State University and The American University in Cairo. I was awarded a Fulbright scholarship to continue studying Arabic in Jordan after graduation. Before returning to the United States, I traveled to Thailand, Malaysia, and Singapore. I was deeply impressed by the energy and creativity of Southeast Asia.

I had been accepted to the University of Michigan's MBA/MA in Middle Eastern Studies program before leaving for Jordan. Shortly after arriving in Ann Arbor, I spoke with Professor Linda Lim and decided to switch to the MBA/MA in Southeast Asian Studies program with a focus on Thai language. I found the program a rewarding and balanced course of study. The students in the joint degree programs were an interesting group. All were acquiring management skills to apply to the regional expertise they were gaining in area studies programs. It was stimulating and refreshing to move between the different worlds of the business school and area studies centers and draw on the perspectives of each.

A Southeast Asia Business Program grant allowed me to spend a summer in Thailand to do research for my master's thesis. I was able to leverage that into an internship with FMC Corp. doing market research for a couple of their businesses there. I learned a great deal from my boss, an old Southeast Asia hand from the U.K. who came to Thailand as a young man. I befriended a Thai businessman at a Thai Board of Investment event sponsored at U-M by the Southeast Asia Business Program the previous semester. Over many meals with him I got great insights into how local businesses worked.

I returned to Michigan to complete my final year of study and write my thesis on the competitiveness of the Thai petrochemical industry. With the help of Foreign Language and Area Studies scholarships, I continued to build on my Thai language skills and establish a competency in Indonesian and Vietnamese at U-M and the Southeast Asian Studies Summer Institute.

After graduation, I took a job at the Monroe Auto Equipment subsidiary of Tenneco in their North American marketing group. It was a great opportunity to learn how a business worked and understand the challenges the company faced in developing markets like Mexico. About the time that it was clear I would not be transferred to Asia with Tenneco, I got a lead from Professor Lim on a job at Dole Packaged Foods.

Dole had an established development program that started with an operations analysis and planning role in California and led to positions at its canning operations in the Philippines and Thailand. They were delighted to find someone with Thai language skills. A month after I started, the company reorganized and the program vanished, but I spent three enjoyable years in southern California developing operations and financial analysis skills. There was management interest in sending me to Thailand after I had some exposure to those operations but no agreement on my role, so nothing happened.

At that point, I returned to Tenneco, where my former boss had become the global VP of Marketing and needed someone in Asia. I moved to Singapore to perform a variety of regional marketing roles. My activities varied according to the needs of the individual countries, which differed dramatically by the maturity of the market and the local Tenneco presence. I spent half my time working with Tenneco's American manufacturing centers to produce export products for East and Southeast Asian markets. The rest of my time was focused on a joint venture in India upgrading their products and launching them under the Monroe brand there.

After three years with Tenneco, I moved back to a finance and operations role by taking a job as Intel's Internal Audit Manager for Asia. Moving into a more senior but narrower job in a tightly managed environment was a challenging experience, but I adapted quickly.

After two years at Intel, I did an honest assessment of my 10 years' experience in the corporate world and determined that, aside from my time in the field in Asia, I found it mostly dissatisfying. My wife, however, enjoyed her marketing career. We agreed that I would pursue my interest trading futures, and we would make decisions based on the needs of her career. That quickly brought us back to California in 2002 when she got a job at Intel headquarters in Silicon Valley.

Since then I have focused on futures trading, stock investing, generating income with options, and generally managing our lives. Although Asia does not figure so prominently in my life, it shaped some of my most important personal relationships. My wife of over 20 years, Amy, is another Asian Studies joint degree graduate whom I met during my time at U-M, and most of my closest friendships were established during my time in Asia.

LEANN ERIKSSON—CJS 1991

Yes, I'm the one who grew up in a small farming community in Iowa. More specifically, my parents' farm was about 10 km from the nearest village of 150 people, in Chester Township, right smack on the border with Minnesota. Five of us lived on a piece of land the size of which housed over 70,000 where I later lived in Tokyo! We lived in a pocket of culture most people only see in movies—think Garrison Keillor's *Prairie Home Companion*—and on top of that, my grandfather was a recent immigrant from Sweden, and grandma's family had arrived in the early 20th century. This taught me to morph easily between different cultures and ways of being.

I spent all of my youth yearning to get out and experience the big world. I read voraciously about history, geography, anthropology, and sociology. Asia was almost completely missed in my formal education. I was studying French at the University of Iowa and realized that, although I absolutely loved learning and speaking it, I wanted more of a challenge. I knew that to become fluent, immersion was the best path. In 1982, the USSR was the evil empire, China wasn't open yet, and I had no calling to go and live in Saudi Arabia as a young, blonde woman—which left Japan. I began my love affair with Japanese in 1983, moved there, and got a job with the Japan Health Center Corporation (JHCC) in 1985 (from an ad in the Mainichi daily news!), and since then, the Japanese language and culture has informed my way of being in ways I'm still realizing today ... more on that below.

Working at JHCC, I saw that there was a way to combine my interest in people and creativity with the business world, so I investigated which grad programs had dual degrees in humanities and business. The University of Michigan's MBA/MA came up as the program with equal strength and offerings on both sides of the degree. The University of California, Berkeley was just beginning their joint degree, and the climate in the Bay

Area appealed, so I applied to both. Michigan offered me a FLAS Fellowship, so my decision was made.

During business school, I got stars in my eyes about the jet-setting, fast-paced, economically rich life of an international business consultant, so when I landed a job consulting at Bain & Company's Tokyo office, I was sure I'd reached heaven. Although I loved the variety of working in many industries and cross-culturally, after several years of physically and mentally crushing hours (and after I'd paid off my grad school loans!), I saw that what mattered most to me were questions bigger than how to improve the bottom lines of large corporations. I took a break from the paid workplace to have two daughters, and this gave me the chance to return to music, one of my greatest loves, and dive into the questions that matter to me: Who are we and what are we here for? What's going on here on Earth? Where are we going? I switched from reading fiction to non-fiction: quantum physics, epigenetics, philosophy, nutrition, alternate "histories," and human potential. I began going to workshops and meeting people who were exploring the aforementioned questions.

What I learned both disturbed and inspired me. The truth of how unsustainable our Western human lifestyle is, and where our world seems to be heading, was depressing. At the same time, I began to see "outside the box" to understand that everything is possible and that I create reality by how I choose to see it. Einstein wisely stated, "We cannot solve our problems with the same thinking we used when we created them." The reason our lifestyle isn't sustainable is that we believe that we are disconnected from the rest of life on this planet. I learned in Japan how humans can be part of larger groups together, intuitively tuning in and knowing that the movement of one affects all. Animals in the wild know instinctively how and when to move, as birds can fly in huge flocks without crashing, and elephants all head for higher ground before tsunamis. We humanimals have this same, innate knowing … children and indigenous peoples live and move with it.

I wrote my master's thesis partially about the story of liquid crystal display technology. It was a foreshadowing. In 2006, I discovered musical instruments called crystal singing bowls, originally created by the computer industry as crucibles in which to grow silicon quartz crystal wafers. It turns out that sound from the singing bowls, especially when combined in specific ways, puts our brains into theta waves. This is the state we're in during dreams, trances, and hypnosis. It's also the state most brains are in between birth and age six or seven, which is why kids learn so easily. It's deeply relaxed, open ... empty and fully receiving. Zen. This is where Japan comes back in.

I haven't lived in Japan since 2003, and diving back into Japanese in the past few years, I see the beauty of the language and culture with new eyes. So many phrases used on a daily basis, and the structure of the language itself, demonstrate the elegantly still, empty, and collective qualities of Zen. For example, *arigatou*, which translates as "thank you," actually means "this is rare" or "this is difficult to exist" (*ari*, "exist" and *katai*, "difficult"). No individual you or me, simply a recognition of something received. Another example is the word *tadaima*, spoken when crossing the threshold into one's home. The usual translation is "I'm home." The Kanji used to write this as "simply now." Home, in the power of now.

I began writing music using the bowls, voice, flutes, and other instruments and have published several CDs as part of Wavegarden and Deep Wild Stillness. My most recent CD is titled *Tadaima* in recognition of its spontaneous creation, coming from stillness and nothingness in the mysterious home of now, the all.

The most recent part of this journey includes spending time with indigenous peoples in various parts of the world, including in Latin America and Africa, and experiencing the wise ways ancient cultures live in harmony in their natural surroundings. Sitting with Himba women in northern Namibia, covered with red ochre and animal fat, bare-breasted and wearing something like 14 kg of skins, shells, and a metal girdle, I was welcomed into their collective field of powerful, grounded women. Ancient peoples hold the key to how we humanimals can step out of our modern boxes and solve our "problems" from a completely different mindset. We humans have learned how to make molecules ... and following nature's lead, how much more creative this is when the collective nature we live in is followed.

My partner and I lead playshops called Voice Awakening that guide participants into expression of their whole voices and beings. This requires a willingness to die to any previous definitions of self, to look into the shadowy places we don't want to own, and realize that each of us is a tiny fragment of the hologram of reality, containing all. I am Donald Trump, and I have created him to show me whom I am. Strong medicine!

The story I've written here doesn't matter. I put in facts to make it more accessible to you. It's a doorway to the path that opens before me and you now and calls us to what's next. It's up to you to find your own way, with what's here. What is calling? Who is here to play with? Where is the greatest joy? How are you giving back, with what you're receiving? What wants to come through when nothing is stopping you? Nothing is in the way except ideas. What ideas do you choose to define your world?

Writing this has led me to revisit this story and see again how perfect the path has been, how seemingly insane decisions make sense in hindsight. *Arigatou* to Linda Lim, who has been an enormous inspiration and support on this journey, for creating the chance to express all of this.

JOE OSHA—CJS 1992

It's hard to believe that it's been 25 years since I left Ann Arbor. I still remember my experience there fondly, and I'm glad to report that I'm still in touch with several of my joint degree classmates. And, of course, married to a Michigan law grad whom I met through a mutual friend while studying Japanese. We're hoping to come for the Ohio State game this year now that we might actually stand a shot at winning.

After graduating from the joint MBA/MA in East Asian Studies program in 1992, I ended up working for Baring Securities in Tokyo as an equity research analyst. When I interviewed for the job, I actually had no idea what an equity research analyst did, but heck, it sounded like fun so off I went. My very patient fiancée, Stephanie, who was working in New York at the time, joined me in Tokyo, and we spent the next five years there. As some of you may recall, Barings went bankrupt in a trading scandal after the 1995 Kobe earthquake, and I moved to another British brokerage—Smith New Court—which was bought by Merrill Lynch later that same year.

By 1997, we decided that we'd had enough of Japan and moved to New York, where I worked for Merrill Lynch as an equity analyst covering semiconductors. We were in New York until 2000—our daughter Margaret was born in 1999—at which point we moved to the San Francisco Bay Area. Our son Gregory arrived in 2001, and I managed to survive as an equity analyst through the tech bust, 9-11, and all of the assorted other fireworks.

By 2007, covering semiconductors was getting to be a bit repetitive, and I took an offer from Merrill Lynch to head up their equity research efforts in Asia. Our family moved to Hong Kong, where we spent the next four years. It was a super experience, and we took full advantage of the opportunity to travel with our family all over Asia. I survived the 2008 crash and subsequent purchase of Merrill by Bank of America, and by 2011 it was getting time to head back to the United States after it became clear that U.S. banks were not going to make the inroads into China that we had hoped for.

I spent another 18 months covering alternative energy for Bank of America in the United States, and another 6 months in management, at which point I decided that the big company management thing wasn't quite for me. I left in 2013 to become the CFO of a start-up company that was focused on rolling up hydropower assets. It was fascinating, challenging work. It became clear after a while that we were going to have to move to Boulder as the company continued to grow, and instead I decided to shift to another start-up, this one focused on development stage technology in geothermal energy. We worked on that technology for about a year, and although it was interesting, it also became apparent that the development path was going to take a lot longer than expected.

In 2016, I joined a mid-sized investment bank—JMP Group—based in San Francisco, and I'm working on industrial and energy technology as an analyst. I really enjoy being an analyst again, especially at a smaller, focused firm. I've spent the last year talking to start-up companies and learning about technology, and it's been super.

I can't say enough about what a fantastic job Linda has done keeping this group together and in touch. With 25 years of perspective behind me, I can say that she is one of the best educators I've ever encountered.

ANDREW MASTERMAN—CJS 1993

After graduation, I moved to Oregon and met my wife, Cheryl. We have been married for 20 years this year (married in 1997 in Portland, Oregon) and have three boys—Zachary (16), Nicholas (14), and Ryan (12)—and one dog (Duffy the Labradoodle). It has been a whirlwind for the past couple of decades, living in Portland (OR), Sendai (Japan), Tokyo, Tucson (AZ), St. Louis (MO), Columbia (SC), and now Philadelphia (PA). Each move has been for work, and several have been changing companies. There have been different organizations, most involving manufacturing, but the most recent in landscaping services. Almost all have involved a great deal of travel, much of it internationally.

Japan has been a part of almost every position, and the education from Michigan in Asian culture and business has proved to be incredibly valuable. Having at the very least a surface level understanding of Asian cultures and the dynamics of Asian history, business, and daily life has allowed me to interact with people with a degree of perspective. Whether in business negotiations or a casual business dinner, showing a proficiency in a region helps to establish credibility. In addition, whether on business or pleasure, the lifelong pursuit of engaging in a foreign culture has added an unquestionable depth to my understanding of the world and continues to open my eyes to its overall wonder.

While I haven't been able to stay in contact with everyone from my years in Ann Arbor, the group of joint degree students and university professors who were in the Asian studies programs from 1990–1993 created one of the best friendship circles of my life. The 10 or 15 of us shared classes, dinners, drinks, and so many other experiences that it created an unbreakable bond of memories that I cherish to this day. We lived in a window of change in both the United States and Asia, as Japan economically peaked and China emerged from decades of self-imposed cultural isolation. Not to mention that expanding beyond the Japan/China juggernauts and taking serious time to explore Southeast Asia, Korea, and the growing influence of India further expanded this perspective. Learning both from books and countless hours of classroom and study sessions in Ann Arbor, combined with on-the-ground exposure in Asia, the band of Asian studies students and professors were a cohort who mutually opened the eyes of all they touched. What a time to be exposed to such a dynamic!

As we now live in another time of unchartered change and uncertainty, I can only hope there are new groups of students who will be the bridges between Asia and America.

TOM STANLEY—CCS (BA, MBA) 1993

My family has always been far-flung. I grew up in Michigan,

mostly, but have always had relatives living and working abroad and traveling to interesting places overseas.

My Aunt Diane in particular was a legendary globetrotter. She had been a journalist and later worked for the U.S. foreign service; in 1978, while assigned to Kathmandu, she joined a small group of Westerners on a three-week trip to the PRC. She shared her impressions and photos from her trip, and I'm sure this is one reason behind my decision in my sophomore year at U-M (fall 1985) to sign up for Chinese 101. At the time, Japanese was "hot"; Chinese was not.

After a year with Professor Tao (and John DeFrancis), I realized that while I found the language fascinating, what I really wanted was to go to China myself to experience the country firsthand. At that time U-M had no study abroad programs in the PRC, but somehow, in those pre-internet days, I learned that the University of Massachusetts had a well-established program for Chinese language study in Taiwan and the PRC. I signed up and spent my junior year abroad, studying at Tunghai University in Taiwan for a summer and at Beijing Normal University for a full academic year (1986–1987).

It was a fascinating time to be in China. The effects of the opening up and reform measures were only just starting to make an impact. I spent as much time as possible traveling the country, visiting almost 20 provinces by train (mostly hard seat), plus a January trip to Tibet that involved four days on a train and two days in a Jiefang truck. I have kept in touch with many of the other students and some of us are planning a 30th reunion in Amherst, Massachusetts, this summer.

I returned to U-M for my senior year. After graduation (BA Asian Languages and Cultures) and a couple of months of unfocused job hunting, I bought a one-way ticket to Taiwan. I started teaching English and later joined KPMG's Taipei office as their English editor. After over two years in Taiwan, I decided to go back to school: I applied to the U-M MBA program and was back in Ann Arbor for two years (1991–1993).

In that distant "pre-global economy" era, the mindset and focus of U.S. business was much more insular and inward looking than today, and the MBA program (including students) reflected this.

After graduation I wanted a China-related job and found a position with a U.S. manufacturing company that had set up a joint venture (JV) in Jiangsu Province, about three hours by road from Shanghai (now 40 minutes away by high-speed rail). They needed a Finance Director: I signed up in January 1994 and found myself back in China for the next two years. I was based in an emerging third tier city, where I lived in a small "foreign expert" apartment in the shadow of our factory on the north bank of the Grand Canal.

Our JV partner was a state-owned enterprise in the traditional mold, and I ended up taking on a marketing role in addition to my FD role. Through "paying my tuition" at the factory for two years I learned a lot about how to do business in China—and some salutary lessons on mistakes to avoid.

After two years, I was ready for a change and moved to Hong Kong. I re-joined KPMG, in the Management Consulting division. Hong Kong was still very much the gateway city for China then, and I focused on strategy consulting and China market entry projects; I later ran our government consulting practice there. My wife, Tina, and I were in Hong Kong for the "handover"; both our children were born there; we all survived a very scary few months of the SARS epidemic.

Of course, China's economy and FDI business were booming in the "aughts," and KPMG's China offices were also growing by leaps and bounds. I put my hand up to move to Shanghai in 2004 with our Deal Advisory team: I worked mainly on inbound M&A transactions and enjoyed the frenetic pace of the "deal environment."

I eventually left the deal team to help set up KPMG's Global China Practice in 2010; we had seen that China was on the cusp of becoming a major outbound investor, so we established a network to better serve Chinese clients as they expanded outside China. It was instructive to see the advice we gave Western investors that came to China in the 1990s being repurposed for the new wave of Chinese outbound investors . . .

In the past few years, I've taken on some new roles (still with KPMG), in our Markets team and as Chief Knowledge Officer for China. These are national roles and have given me the chance to work across all our business units and regions in China and to work directly with our regional and global leadership.

It's unusual these days to have stayed with the same company for an entire career, but that's how it worked out for me. Within the same firm I've worked across a number of very different roles and teams, so it has never felt stale. I absolutely credit the broad background and skills I developed at Michigan as the main reason that I have been a versatile player on the KPMG bench in China.

In the past few years (largely through the efforts of Professor Lim!), I've been pleased to renew and extend my U-M connections in Shanghai and Ann Arbor, especially since 2015 when my daughter started her freshman year at U-M Ann Arbor. She is in East Quad, across the street from the expanded new Ross campus.

Many thanks to Professor Lim for the chance to share my personal story–and Go Blue!

NANCY YU–CCS 1994

I grew up mainly in Alabama, but my father was born in Guangzhou and immigrated first to Hong Kong and then to the United States to attend college and medical school. I made my first trip to the PRC in 1984 with my dad, when we visited his birthplace, our relatives, and many major cities in his first visit back since the late 1940s. I studied Chinese and comparative area studies (focus on China) at Duke University and spent a year working in Taiwan after graduating. While pursuing the dual degree program at U-M, I had the opportunity to serve as a

Davidson Institute internship fellow through which we spent the summer in Chongqing working at Dongfeng Motor Corporation (one of the large state-owned auto companies).

My first job after graduation was working as a manager in the China Strategy Group at Coopers and Lybrand Consulting (now PwC). My team was based in Shanghai, and I regularly traveled between my NYC base and client sites in Greater China, including Beijing, Taipei, Hong Kong, Chongqing, and Shanghai. Although I started as a generalist, I developed an expertise in the pharmaceuticals industry through an extended engagement working on the Asian integration of the merger between two global corporations.

Although I transitioned into the healthcare investing world, I maintain a strong interest in China and continued studying Mandarin on my own for much of that time. I worked in equity research covering the pharmaceutical industry for over 10 years and currently work as a biopharma industry and financial analyst in the Center for Health Policy and Outcomes at Memorial Sloan-Kettering Cancer Center.

I am married to Jody Kochansky and have four kids, ranging from 8 (twin girls!) to 16 years old. I am active in my community and school, including serving on the Board of the Bronxville School Foundation and as treasurer of the Bronxville Middle School Council.

MICHAEL LITTLE—CCS 1994

If hot, steamy river deltas where people eat rice and seafood sounds like a description of Shanghai or Bangkok, then it could just as easily describe where I am from, New Orleans, Louisiana. But how do you get from the levees on the Mississippi to the bund on the Huangpu?

When I was growing up, Asia was as far away as you can go from Louisiana. Sumatra and Borneo were exotic names of places I never thought I would visit. So what got me over to Asia? I have to blame it all on Virgil.

I studied Latin in high school and did well until I started the *Aeneid*. That was when I realized that dactylic hexameter (yes, I had to look that up) was not my future. So I looked around for another language to study, and I chose Chinese because it was as far from Latin as you can get.

One year of Mandarin in high school and over the summer of 1985, I had the chance to study at Fudan University in Shanghai. I remember an outing to the No. 10 Department Store. I was shown the "watch department"—six watches in a 12-inch-long display case. I thought: this place is crazy; I have to come back!

I attended Oberlin College (based on their strength in teaching undergraduate Chinese), and while there I spent my junior year abroad at Peking University, where I really learned to speak Mandarin. I graduated from college in the weeks after Tiananmen Square with a degree in Chinese Language and Literature. As you can imagine, the future was a bit unclear at that time. So I took a chance in 1990 and returned to China to teach English to graduate students at the Guangdong Academy of Sciences.

While in Guangzhou I knew that I wanted to continue working in and with Asia but that I needed to take a further step. A BA in Chinese Lit was not enough. I took the GRE and applied to several programs including the University of Michigan Asian Studies program. I was fortunate to finish the MA coursework in one year, but felt that an MA in Asian Studies really leads either to a PhD or an MBA. I joined the joint degree program in 1992 and graduated with dual degrees (MA Asian Studies and MBA) in 1994, having written a thesis on transportation in China.

The MAP program at the business school was only fully launched my first year of business school, and I worked with Cummins Engine on a project in Michigan in preparation for a summer internship with the William Davidson Institute in Chongqing, China.

The business school was much different then. Business students had less real-world work experience, teamwork was "in," and MAP had just started. And the computer lab was a social hub. You worked there because no one had computers at home. No more.

In 1994, I was hired by Carrier Corp., a part of United Technologies, for their leadership program. That year Carrier was focused on hiring folks with Asian experience and hired a number of MBAs who were Asian or had backgrounds in Chinese and Japanese area studies.

Carrier had me work in the United States for a year before heading off to Shanghai, Singapore, and Hong Kong for six years. While I had started with a focus on China, I was fortunate to travel across the region and ended up as regional IT manager with responsibility from Japan to India to New Zealand and all parts in between.

But that path was not a straight one. I started in marketing, then dealer development, then export logistics followed by IT. It was not until 2001, when I started work on low-cost sourcing in China, that I began to work in the area where I have been ever since: purchasing.

Why purchasing? One of the funny things about big American corporations is the operating assumption that "the world is flat," that business is business everywhere. But there are niches where "knowing" about the rest of the world is valuable. And purchasing is one of those niches. The Executive Global VP of Purchasing doesn't want to know that all purchase orders in China and Vietnam need a company "chop" to be legal, but someone has to have that knowledge and be able to explain the strange nuances and practices of buying overseas.

For many years I felt the MBA and the Asian Studies MA were opposites. The MBA teaches quantitative analysis, statistics, bean counting, and project management, all driven by data. The MA teaches induction from scraps of knowledge and working with data that has to be mined and interpreted and reasoned into prose arguments. MBAs do bullets points. MAs write books. How do you bring the two together?

Carefully. As an area studies major, I am always amazed by the general lack of what I consider basic knowledge: Why can't my Indian team all eat the same food/meat? What is a *hukou*? And why do Chinese not like Japan? So there is value in bringing the area knowledge into the world of business (yes, the project in Indonesia requires a prayer room on premises . . .) and a role to play being that guide and explorer. But it is not easy.

Happily, most of the purchasing people I have worked for believe that the world is not flat, that local knowledge is critical to success, that every day is new in Asia, and that solutions are cut from the whole cloth but tailored to places in Asia and the rest of the world.

I am now a father of four and have just relocated to Bangkok, Thailand, after living many years in Shanghai, China, where every day brings something exciting.

PAUL CHURCHILL—CSEAS 1994

I grew up a somewhat typical "third-culture kid": born in Manila to an American father and Filipina mother, I spent my babyhood in Jakarta, preschool in Washington, DC, primary school in Manila, and high school in Australia. I guess that background is what sparked my interest in international affairs. But it meant that when I moved to the United States as a teenager, I was in many ways a stranger in my own country.

I attended college in the United States, and although I enjoyed getting to know the American side of my identity, in my early twenties, I decided it was only a matter of time before I headed back to Asia. When I discovered that Michigan offered a combined MBA/MA program, with a focus on exactly the region I wanted to study (Southeast Asia), the decision was an easy one.

And indeed, it was a great fit. The MBA courses gave me a foundation for success in the business world that my more academically oriented parents could not, while the MA courses provided a bridge to a region that I found both fascinating and familiar. The chance to balance my marketing, finance, and accounting lectures with anthropology, history, geography, and language courses was a great combination, even if it meant that my classmates doing their respective MBAs or MAs did not really understand what the other half was all about.

During my three years in Ann Arbor, I had the chance to re-learn Bahasa Indonesia—a language I had grown up speaking like a local my first four years but that I eventually lost when we left Jakarta. It opened the doors to a summer internship in Indonesia, with it the thrill of being able to converse with everyone from local managers to waiters and shopkeepers—giving me a deeper connection to the culture than many of the longer-serving expat managers had experienced. (To this day, I remain grateful for the FLAS scholarship that enabled such language lessons and still carry a degree of guilt for not having leveraged this into a more Asia-focused career afterwards.)

I also had the chance to witness live the evolution of today's acclaimed Asia Business Conference. I was part of a group of students that built upon the already successful Japan Business Conference, turned it into a Southeast Asian Business Conference one year, and then finally re-badged it as the broader Asia Business Conference in my final year.

Other memories include International Business Club meetings and potluck dinners, the thrill of having my MA thesis on economic development in Penang and Cebu published, attending an InterPacific Conference on Phuket, a post-graduation Asia study tour to Hong Kong and Jakarta, and non-academically, enjoying firsthand a few glory years of Michigan sports (basketball's Fab Five and football's Desmond Howard at the same time!).

Needless to say, my most treasured memories were the friends I made during those years, with none more inspirational than Professor Linda Lim. Like many others, I took her classic Business in Asia course and thoroughly enjoyed it. But what I really treasured were the discussions outside the classroom, her guidance on my master's thesis, and her leadership of the dual degree program. She was much more than a professor, taking the time to coach us as we organized club events and conferences; opening doors to internships, scholarships, and job opportunities; and becoming a friend by opening her and Pete Gosling's house to regular get-togethers.

Despite everything lined up for a career in Asia, fate would intervene at one of those above-mentioned International Business Club potluck dinners. In my final year in Ann Arbor, I met an attractive Austrian exchange student at one of those events, and she would later become my wife. My planned move to Asia was derailed by a post-graduation move to Vienna, where we both said that after a couple of years, we would still head out together to Southeast Asia.

Even though that remained the plan for several years, bit by bit other life events intervened, and our Asia plans became less concrete. My curiosity for international experiences took on a European dimension, as my career opportunities took us from Vienna to Geneva and then Frankfurt, Cambridge, Nuremberg, and Munich. At least when the chance arose, I became the "Asian guy" and enjoyed various business trips to Southeast Asia, China, and Japan over the years.

My own third-culture children have grown up bilingually, speaking English and German since birth, but our family food of choice, ironically, remains Asian. They say, "an apple never falls far from the tree," and I guess those family trips to visit Philippine beaches, plus their grandmother's home cooking, have left their mark!

After 20+ years here, I feel more European these days than anything. But every time I visit family in the Philippines or some other part of Southeast Asia on a business trip, I still feel very much "at home" with the food, culture, and way of life. One of our good friends has just moved from Munich to Singapore and keeps urging us to follow. The journey is not yet over, so who knows, perhaps the road less traveled will still result in an Asian chapter ...

JAY YOSHIOKA—CSEAS 1994

I am fortunate to have grown up in Kailua, Hawaii, which boasts one of the most picturesque beaches in the world and one you've undoubtedly seen in films and travel photos. My paternal great-grandparents and maternal great-great-grandparents immigrated to Hawaii from Japan during the reign of the Meiji Emperor. As a third-generation Japanese-American on one side of my family and a fourth-generation on the other, I was raised speaking not much other than English and Hawaiian pidgin English. In high school, I studied Spanish and had no interest in studying Japanese or any other Asian language.

During my first year at Pitzer College, I met a group of students from Japan who conversed often in Japanese. I remember feeling frustrated that I couldn't understand what they were saying half of the time, so in my second year, I enrolled in my first Japanese language class and in a Japanese literature in translation class at Pomona College. The more I studied, the more intrigued I became because I started to understand context through language. I recall reading Yukio Mishima's Sea of Fertility tetralogy and for some reason was fascinated by the third novel, *Temple of Dawn,* which is the namesake of a famous Bangkok temple, Wat Arun. I became so motivated to further my Japanese that I spent my third year in a study abroad program at Waseda University in Tokyo. During a long school break there, I ventured to Thailand for the first time and immediately felt a familiarity with it.

After college, I moved to Japan and taught English for several years, first in a rural area and then in Tokyo. While there I visited Thailand again and realized I wanted to live there and to learn the language. I moved to Bangkok, studied Thai and traveled and fell absolutely in love with the country. My experiences in Thailand made me realize I wanted to pursue an advanced degree in Thai studies and a practical degree that would enable my language ability. I started my school search from Bangkok and focused on Thai studies programs at schools with top-rated MBA programs. My requirements narrowed my search to UC Berkeley, Cornell, and Michigan. I ultimately chose Michigan because of its integrated joint MBA/MA in Asian Studies program and because its Thai language program was taught by a native Thai speaker.

I am a strong believer in the joint degree program because it marries language (the vehicle), cultural understanding (the context), and business (the acumen). I was challenged at Ross and stimulated at Rackham. The students, faculty, staff, and approaches at the schools were different, but courses such as Linda Lim's Business in Asia melded the disciplines extremely well. I enjoyed the Center for Southeast Asian Studies because it brought students from the various schools together and created multifaceted discussions and events. As for language learning, I was very fortunate to have studied in-country while learning Japanese and Thai. I believe there is no substitute for learning a language in-country.

Michigan offered much in terms of experiences. In my second year of the three-year program, I studied in Milan at Bocconi University's SDA Graduate School of Management because I wanted to learn about the EC (European Community), the precursor to the EU (European Union). I also spent two summers doing internships in Singapore and in Bangkok.

My MA thesis was on the growth of the Southeast Asian airline industry. Not so coincidentally, I was recruited by Northwest Airlines (now Delta Airlines) in Minneapolis-St. Paul, where I started in Asia-Pacific route planning. I recall putting myself on the airline's Finance and Marketing recruiting schedules and was interviewed by Robert Isom (current President of American Airlines) and Charles Breer (current Managing Director at Alaska Airlines and fellow Ross School alum). After Northwest Airlines, I was at Cendant Corporation's RCI Division in New Jersey, where I managed global marketing focused mainly on the U.S. and European markets. After September 11, 2001, the travel industry suffered greatly, so in 2002, I went to work for Wells Fargo Bank in San Francisco, and my focus shifted to U.S. domestic business.

While I feel I've had a good career with great experiences, I do think I should have pursued opportunities in Asia and/or at companies with strong Asia business ties.

Recently, I have been thinking about a career change focused on eldercare and/or with an organization with Asia ties. Aside from work, I've been spending more time giving back to the community through volunteer work and resource support in San Francisco and Thailand. I have been a supporter of the Thai Language Endowment and the Amnuay Virawan Fund at U-M. I also spend a lot of time traveling and am in Asia regularly.

I met many interesting people at Rackham and Ross and developed some long-lasting friendships. The people who most influenced me at U-M were Professor Linda Lim at the business school and Montatip Krishnamra, my Thai language instructor.

I am fortunate.

DREW KRAISINGER—CSEAS 1995

I grew up in a small town southeast of Pittsburgh, Pennsylvania, where Asia and Asian culture seemed so far away, yet in the 1970s and 1980s, international trade dynamics impacted the region's steel mills dramatically. With a desire to see the world, I spent a year in Belgium as an exchange student learning Flemish and Dutch and experienced many countries in Europe riding the rails. It also gave me an on-the-ground view of international politics impacting local communities as the Reagan administration deployed Pershing II missiles in communities around me.

In studying foreign affairs at the University of Virginia, I got a chance to expand my view and learn about the rapid economic growth of the Asian Tigers. Soon study abroad at the National University of Singapore gave me exposure to the politics, history, and developing economies in Southeast Asia. I think most impactful were my experiences traveling that brought the lessons of the classroom to life. For example, during a school break, while traveling across Java to Bali and back, I experienced how the overnight 40% devaluation of the rupiah impacted many people, especially those who had so little. Later, I traveled from Singapore by bus, train, and boat up Peninsular Malaysia to the top of Northern Thailand and back again. The geography, local culture, and the pragmatic nature of the communities along the trip impressed me greatly.

After finishing up at UVA, I worked in information systems for a few years, but the lure of Asia remained. One of my best friends from Singapore at that time was studying sociology at the University of Michigan. Knowing my interests, she introduced me to Linda Lim and Pete Gosling.

I remember how tremendously Pete and Linda championed Southeast Asian studies at the University. I was excited and grateful for the opportunity to pursue the joint MBA/MA in Asian Studies. Being awarded a Foreign Language and Area Studies scholarship helped make it possible.

Pete, Linda, and many others at the Center for Southeast Asian Studies were immensely helpful in teaching and connecting a community of people with shared interests at Michigan and beyond. One of my more memorable experiences was learning Bahasa Indonesia at the Southeast Asian Studies Summer Institute (SEASSI) at the University of Washington in the summer of 1992. We were a tight knit group of students and teachers who immersed ourselves in Bahasa nearly 24/7.

The next summer, I did two internships focused on the telecommunication industry in emerging or transitional economies in Poland and Indonesia. These internships were made possible in part by the William Davidson Institute at the University of Michigan. These experiences helped lay the foundation for my MA thesis on telecommunications development in Indonesia.

After graduation at Michigan, I was ready to take a job in

information systems consulting when connections brought forward a different opportunity. Linda and Paul Churchill pointed to me as a possible candidate for General Motors to help them start up their new regional Asia Pacific operations in Singapore. It was a match that I could not pass up, especially because my best friend from Singapore was soon to become my wife. The job with GM took me to most countries in the region and frequently to Thailand. I helped lead a team that built a greenfield assembly plant southeast of Bangkok. Undeterred by the Asian financial crisis in 1997, we launched a new car for export, the first vehicle out of GM's new plant in Rayong, Thailand, in record time.

After about five years working in Asia and Australia, I headed back to Michigan to expand my product development and marketing experience with GM. Even though I was no longer directly responsible for operations in Asia, I often was called on to help guide GM projects in Asia, Australia, and other regions.

About eight years ago, I made a career switch to focus on innovation in the health insurance and IT industry. As my many experiences in Asia taught me, success is about applying a pragmatic spirit to generate things that create trust and value. Today, working with a software-as-service and analytics company, I get to pioneer new offerings and build value for people every day. I never seem to run out of market challenges and business problems to solve, especially around engaging consumers in their health and care.

I continue to have a strong interest in Southeast Asia and love to visit with family and friends in the region. I have been fortunate to cross paths with fellow joint degree alums, in Asia and elsewhere around the world. It is amazing how the bonds of learning a language together, doing business school projects, or sharing Asian studies classes last. The joint degree program at the University of Michigan has been life changing. Friendships from the immersive experiences of learning Bahasa Indonesia at

SEASSI continue to this day. Thank you, Pete, for suggesting that I do it!

My experience in the University of Michigan joint MBA/MA in Asian Studies program has helped me make a difference in every place in the world that I have landed.

ARIF IQBALL—CJS 1995

In 1981, at 17 years of age, I left Pakistan, the country that I was born in, to live and study in the United States—a decision that greatly impacted my ability to learn and grow and to become a contributing member of society. Eighteen years later, in 1999, I left the United States for Japan with a dual degree (MBA/MA in Japanese Studies) from the University of Michigan to spend the next third of my life unlearning my Western style of working and relearning how to contribute in a Japanese environment.

In Pakistan, I learned tradition and Asian values and an Eastern way of thinking. In the United States, my education and work experience provided me with a very Western approach to life and work. It was those sometimes opposing perspectives that first got me interested in Japan because (viewed from a distance) it had a balance of both tradition and modernism as well as Eastern and Western elements that function well with each other.

Upon graduating with a Master in Engineering from Northwestern University in 1990, I began work as a test engineer crashing cars for Ford Motor Company and decided to pursue my MBA after a few years. For my MBA application essay, I highlighted how I specifically wanted to help Ford expand in Asia, and (in my very first semester) my personal curiosity took me to Tom Roehl's class on Japanese business. To say that class changed my life is appropriate, and I suddenly felt right at home with both a personal and professional vision of what I wanted to do for the rest of my life and career.

The Michigan Business School was already one of the top MBA institutions in the country, but I was pleasantly surprised to find out the strength and reputation of the Center for Japanese Studies as one of the premier institutions for Japan and Japanese language study. With Dr. Roehl's encouragement and support from Dr. John Campbell and the Japan Technology Management Program (JTMP), I received the first of a series of fellowships that allowed me to study Japanese in Japan during the summer of 1993 and for the rest of my studies. Upon my return from Japan, I applied for the dual degree (MBA/MA in Japanese Studies) option and was able to convince both work and school to allow me to work full-time while studying full-time.

I was fortunate to be in the dual degree program at a time when many students were keen on not only taking the extra time to develop new language skills but also taking the risk to start at the ground level in their chosen countries of interest. If not for the inspiration and support from my teachers at U of M and some great bosses, I would still be working as an engineer in Dearborn.

For my master's thesis, I chose to write (under Dr. Linda Lim and Dr. Mary-Yoko Brannen) about Toyota's new market entry strategy in Thailand and Indonesia. I also presented the thesis at work to Ford's top management, leading to my first overseas assignment in Japan upon graduation in 1995.

That first assignment in Japan was for Ford as part of the first co-located team inside Mazda, which was experiencing severe financial difficulty. Although I was well prepared with my MBA/MA and Japanese language experience, that one-year assignment was perhaps the most difficult experience in my work life; it helped me understand the importance of finance and strategy in adding value to the company and was the basis of my future career in finance.

Upon my return to the United States, I continued to work at Ford and was involved in progressive assignments mostly involving U.S. and European manufacturing sites. In 1999, Makoto Ariga, a Michigan Business School alumnus, invited me to go back to Japan, and I gladly accepted. What was supposed to be a short-term assignment has now grown into an 18 plus year career.

My career has taken me across industries from automotive to direct selling/cosmetics to healthcare to advertising to education and nursing care as well as across functions including finance, strategy, administration, sales support, IT, HR, legal, and procurement. Due to my MBA/MA in Japanese Studies education and language skills, I was able to create a unique value proposition and deliver results that allowed me to gain trust and continue to grow. Most recently, I was one of a handful of foreign CFOs in a Tier 1 publicly traded Japanese company.

I continue to deepen my study of Japanese culture and have been working on a long-term project photographing the elusive Geisha community in Kyoto, recently taking up residence there. Photographs from the project have been published in magazines in Italy, Germany, and the United States, and I am hoping to be able to complete a photobook that does justice to the elegant and sophisticated world of these artists.

If I were to give advice to students looking at the dual degree option and the extra year involved, I would definitely say, take the step, follow your compass and not your clock, believe in your abilities to navigate the difficulties that you will encounter with this acquired knowledge, and emerge as your true self.

I am who I am because of my University of Michigan experience and am eternally grateful. My career evolution, from crashing cars to being the CFO of a public company, is proof that because of the dual degree program, one has access to more opportunities, possibly less competition on a fast track, and ability to wear many different hats in an exciting international career.

NAT SIDDALL—CSEAS 1997

I was one of the earlier joint program students, with an MBA and MA in Southeast Asian Studies, and one of the less successful ones, in terms of subsequent accomplishments. But I have few regrets.

My initial plan was simply to acquire the MBA credential and a bit of language, return to California, thence to Malaysia, and eat well for the rest of my life.

But life's path followed twists and turns such that my graduate degrees have had little practical application. I still pay attention to international news and have an awareness of the world that I would not have without my study at the University of Michigan. I loved being part of the university community and still do to some extent.

Education is a funny thing: always valuable, but not so predictable. For me, accounting and finance courses broadened my mind and enriched my world, more than all the history and philosophy in my fancy liberal arts undergraduate program. But the business and business school world is really not for me. As for language study . . . well, they say it reduces the risk of senile dementia, so that should be becoming valuable soon.

My lifestyle goals changed as I lingered in Ann Arbor, and I settled down in Chelsea, Michigan. I became interested in windsurfing, which had a little potential for a Southeast Asia connection, since Thailand was a center for windsurfer manufacturing. But when I became Executive Director of the US Windsurfing Association, the USWA office moved here, rather than me moving anywhere else.

Windsurfing declined. I still sail but no longer compete and no longer have that job. Now I explore wetlands in western Washtenaw County, looking for native orchids. I've created and maintain a nature preserve on land purchased by Scio Township. Alien invasive Asian species are my great enemy. I think globally but act locally.

My new hobby is backcountry skiing out west.

JYOTHI NAMBIAR DAS—CSAS 1997

I grew up in a Boston suburb, the child of two Indian immigrants from Kerala. Growing up in Massachusetts in the 1980s, there were painfully few Asian immigrants, and I always felt a deep desire to better understand my culture and heritage. I had experienced many of the holidays and traditions as my family worked hard to preserve them. Most of their friends were also immigrants, so I did have an "extended family" of Keralite immigrants. However, I craved a deeper understanding of the politics, history, and language.

This need became stronger for me after I graduated from Swarthmore College with a BA in English Literature and Economics. The distance from my family and cultural network made me realize how much I missed the Indian part of my life. After graduating, I returned to the Boston area and worked in a small policy think tank, expecting to get a degree in public policy. I soon realized that public policy research was not my calling and decided to pursue a business degree, thinking it would open up greater opportunities for me.

I wanted to supplement my business degree with a concentration in South Asia so that I would be able to fulfill my desire to learn more about my heritage. Fortunately, one of my Swarthmore professors introduced me to Linda Lim, his former colleague at Swarthmore, who had moved to the University of Michigan. The university offered a dual Master's in Business Administration and South Asian Studies.

I am forever grateful to this connection as it made my years at Michigan so much richer and satisfying. I was able to get my MBA while deepening my knowledge of South Asian history, culture, and language. I am also indebted to Linda's advice and guidance throughout my graduate studies. She introduced me to internship and scholarship opportunities and made it the most enjoyable educational experience I had ever had.

Linda Lim's International Business course opened my eyes to the intricacies of international trade and the dynamics of doing business abroad. She exposed me to a whole different dimension of business life in Asia. Combining these courses with academic courses in South Asian anthropology, economics, and history completely broadened my understanding of the region.

Linda was so generous in her introductions and connections. She introduced me to Brad Farnsworth of the Center for International Business Education (CIBE) and Ted Snyder of the William Davidson Institute. My experiences working with them helped me to land a summer internship at an electronics company in India and a grant to research the consumer goods distribution system. This research led to an interest in brand management.

After graduating, I worked in brand management at Unilever and met my husband, Jai, who had grown up in India. Much to his father's dismay, he had rejected his admission to the Indian Institute of Technology and instead moved to the United States as an undergraduate. As an IIT professor, his father had often lamented that his best students often left India.

Jai and I moved to California after getting married. I've been fortunate to have a few business projects in Asia throughout my career—I worked on a Japanese product line that brought me to Tokyo and ran a technology pilot in India while working at LexisNexis.

I now have two sons who thankfully have a much more diverse cultural network growing up in the Bay Area than I did in Boston. We've taken them on several trips to India, but now that they are entering middle school, I want them to understand the importance of a true global perspective. Hopefully they will make their grandfather proud and develop a deeper understanding and appreciation of their heritage.

PATRICK J. GRIFFIN—CSEAS 1998

Being born and raised in southern Indiana, I really did not have a chance to learn much about Southeast Asia in my daily life. However, I did have a passionate interest in other cultures, perhaps motivated by my relatives, who had been in the Peace Corps or were involved in international education. I hoped to experience life beyond Indiana and the United States. Taking that first step, I headed to San Antonio, Texas, after high school to attend Trinity University, where I studied history and economics.

My interests in Southeast Asia grew immensely when I had the opportunity to take that second step and work for the U.S. Foreign Commercial Service in Singapore in 1992. My eyes opened immediately to this new and colorful part of the world. Singapore was an exciting place as it was transitioning from Lee Kuan Yew's longtime leadership. My work there focused mainly on writing research reports, assisting with trade fairs, and organizing meetings for U.S. businesses interested in expanding into Singapore and Southeast Asia. I fortunately had the chance to travel around Southeast Asia and begin to learn about its long history and diverse cultures. Over time, I became genuinely fascinated by the region, particularly Singapore, Indonesia, and Malaysia.

I knew that I eventually wanted to go to graduate business school. One day while cataloging newly arrived journals, magazines, and books at the Commercial Service's library in Singapore, I noticed a copy of the *Journal of Southeast Asian Business*, which is now known as the *Journal of Asian Business*. Reading through the journal, I learned about Dr. Linda Lim, the University of Michigan, and the possibility of combining my emerging fascination with Southeast Asia and my keen interest in business. This epiphany really changed my life. I charted a course to hopefully complete a joint degree and launch an international business career focused on the emerging opportunities in Southeast Asia.

Starting the business school application process back in the USA, I visited Ann Arbor over the summer of 1994 and had the chance to meet with Dr. Linda Lim. Her infectious enthusiasm immediately sold me on Michigan as the leading beehive of Southeast Asian business activity among several business schools with joint degree programs. Linda inspired me to apply to the joint degree and counseled me to focus on the business school application, where most of the aspiring joint degree students get tripped up. Following her advice, I applied early and was fortunately accepted. I knew that Michigan was my first choice, which luckily made the business school decision pretty easy at the time.

My wife, Jill, whom I met in college, joined me at Michigan. She had been teaching economics in Bulgaria. She completed a joint degree in business and industrial engineering at U-M and studied Japanese through the Japanese Technology Management Program. Jill and I actually took two gamelan classes together at the Burton Memorial Tower. She has always been the better musician in our family! I finally had the opportunity to introduce Jill to Southeast Asia when we honeymooned in Bali in 1996 during the summer after our first year at Michigan. We hope to get back there again for an anniversary!

We had a diverse and energetic group of joint degree students during the mid- to late 1990s as attested by the many alumni reflections from that era. With Linda's motivation, assistance, and amazing network around the world, we restarted the Asian Business Conference, which has grown tremendously over the years. In organizing the panel discussions, I appreciated the opportunity to interact with business leaders, many of whom were U-M graduates or had strong connections to Ann Arbor.

From getting to know Michael Wachtel my first year at Michigan, a fellow Southeast Asian joint degree student, I learned more about the FLAS Fellowship program at U-M. He counseled me to explore applying to the program. I discussed with Linda and applied for the fellowship for the following academic year. I am grateful and honored to have been awarded the fellowship my last two years at Michigan. This certainly eased the financial burden of attending graduate school. Thanks again Linda and Michael!

Through the Center for International Business Education, I had the opportunity to go on a school trip to the Philippines and South Korea with a group of students and professors. The University of Michigan connections were evident as alumni hosted events and opened doors along our way. One of the highlights of our trip was the chance to meet President Fidel Ramos of the Philippines and Roberto de Ocampo who was Secretary of Finance at the time.

Along with numerous others, I enjoyed the many special parties at Pete and Linda's fascinating house. The food and conversations were sublime particularly with the tranquil setting. Pete and Linda have been genuinely welcoming to so many students over the years.

I feel very fortunate to have taken a class from both Linda and Pete while at the University of Michigan. I thoroughly enjoyed Pete's class and still reflect on the life of Burmese *nats* and Southeast Asia's diverse rice terraces. I continue to appreciate Linda's nuanced perspective on Southeast Asian business, culture, and politics. I have really enjoyed reading her articles in newspapers and magazines over the years. We joint degree students and hangers-on have all been lucky to be graced by her wit and wisdom!

When considering my summer internship opportunities, Linda counseled me to do something interesting in Indonesia rather than a typical MBA internship. I had been on a track to work for Koch Industries or United Technologies. Through her many connections, I was able to line up a summer internship with Rudy Pesik, who is one of the most successful *pribumi* entrepreneurs in Indonesia. At the time, he had a variety of interests including the DHL franchise in Indonesia. Rudy is a colorful person and imparted a unique perspective on doing business in Indonesia. My time in Jakarta also provided a chance for me to practice my Bahasa Indonesia, which I had studied intensively at Arizona State in the Southeast Asian Studies Summer Institute (SEASSI) language program. The summer internship experience also inspired my MA thesis. With Linda as my patient and sage advisor, I wrote my MA thesis on *pribumi* entrepreneurship in Indonesia.

Life takes many twists and turns as we know from these alumni reflections. My life veered away from Southeast Asia after leaving the University of Michigan, perhaps due to timing, luck, or fate. The year 1998 was one of striking contrasts with the Asian economic crisis in full swing and the internet bubble starting to form in the USA.

I began my post-Michigan career at Koch Industries in Wichita, Kansas, and hoped to use that as launching ground for my international business career. Koch had planned to grow its business in Southeast Asia but canceled those plans when commodity prices hit rock bottom partly due to the Asian economic crisis. I began to consider other more entrepreneurial opportunities.

My direction shifted further when I joined a group of ex-Koch employees who started one of the first comparison shopping websites, bottomdollar.com, before Google's ascent. We raised some venture capital, built the business, and successfully sold the company to Network Commerce based in Seattle, Washington.

I eventually returned to southern Indiana in 2002 to work for Escalade, Inc., which is a sporting goods outdoor recreation company. Aside from five years in Germany with one of our subsidiaries, I have been based in Indiana with Jill, raising our children Graham and Greta.

Through my work, I travel to China primarily as a board member on behalf of our joint venture Stiga Sports, which is based in Eskilstuna, Sweden. Drawing on my Asian business and educational experience, I worked closely with the Stiga CEO to successfully transition its business in China from a distributor to a wholly owned subsidiary. We thankfully avoided many pitfalls along the way. Today, Stiga sponsors the Chinese national table tennis team and several top players, including Xu Xin and Fan Zendong, and has a very meaningful table tennis business in China. Stiga is now implementing a similar transition in Japan, which is the second most important table tennis market in the world.

I think about Linda and Pete often and the impact they have had on my life. Linda took the time to mentor me at a pivotal time in my life, and I am forever grateful. Pete imparted a unique framework for better understanding and appreciating the different cultures of Southeast Asia. My life is richer today due to those formative and magical experiences at the University of Michigan.

BOB WILSON—CJS 1998

I want to thank Professor Linda Lim for asking me to provide feedback on a program that literally changed my life, expanding my opportunities by marking me as a person willing to take the road less traveled. The joint degree program at U-M is one of the best investments a person can make in themselves.

I grew up in a military (U.S. Air Force) family and biracial—my Mom is Japanese from Kumomoto-ken, Kyushu. We moved often, and actually I kind of thought of myself as a poor southern boy from Mississippi before moving to Okinawa, Japan, in the seventh grade. For six terrific years, I had the opportunity to experience Japanese culture firsthand from the safety of going home to America on the base. From those formative years, my appreciation for the Japanese lifestyle and my dual mindset began.

For several years after returning stateside, and after graduating from Michigan Technological University with a BS in Chemical Engineering, my focus was on building my career, and my interest in Japan was relegated to finding good Japanese cuisine. In 1993, I was hired by Mitsubishi Rayon to start a business in the United States and lead its marketing, and my fascination grew, not only to explore my own personal identity and heritage but also for business. Through the company's product and technology development efforts, I became fully immersed in business practice; I was hooked.

By 1994, I knew that to progress in my career and to eventually run businesses, further education was necessary. Since business school was in my plans, taking the opportunity to invest in Japanese studies was a natural extension. University of Michigan was high on my list, and became my first choice for three important reasons: (a) the top business school program; (b) a three-year program enabling me more time to spend on both areas; and (c) the Japan Technology Management Program, which gave me a one-year scholarship to fund my extra year.

The education and experiences both on campus and off far exceeded my expectations and helped me grow as a person. With my classmates, I had the best of both worlds—inspirational, driven, and engaged business leaders on the one hand and smart, curious, and dedicated liberal arts post-grads on the other. I came in to the program as an engineer's businessman and through the joint program and learning a little about liberal arts disciplines, came out a balanced person with much greater interests.

What impressed me most was that there was so much depth outside the hard-core business and sciences. I remember really enjoying a premodern history of Japan class and through it grew to better appreciate how business was done in the Tokugawa period. The professors and students stretched my thinking through debates on modern Japanese politics, sociology, and literature. Later in life, these critical thinking skills and different perspectives helped me look beyond the numbers and better manage international leaders and businesses.

One summer in 1996, I had the opportunity to go to Kanazawa, Japan, to take a summer session with the Princeton University language program. It was a tremendous experience with a home-stay family, and I had the opportunity to see much of the prefecture over that summer.

The one area that I could have done more with was language studies. At Michigan, it progressed nicely, but after graduation, I did not enable it to stick. It got extensive use a decade later while running a business from Japan, but it is my one regret that I did not immediately go to Japan after graduation instead of going into consulting.

My thesis was on business cycles within the Japanese chemical industry, and Professor Linda Lim was my advisor on the paper. I had the opportunity to go to Japan on spring break to do some primary research, interviewing many leaders who were involved in the mergers and joint venture companies that were created over various periods of industry expansion and contraction. That trip was also funded by the Japan Technology Management Program.

My first post-degree job was in management consulting with Arthur D. Little (ADL) in Boston. What drove me there was the combination of strategy with specialization in the chemical industry. Although my Japanese studies did not enable work specifically in Japan, most of my cases were international, with a very long assignment in Korea during the "big deal" M&A efforts following the IMF currency crisis of the late 1990s and early 2000s. I interned at ADL the summer of 1997, and my expanded studies were of interest to them.

My career has been an exciting journey. After leaving ADL, I joined a dot-com funded by Kleiner Perkins and helped set up a subsidiary company in Singapore. Later I was part of the team that shut it down. I worked in Silicon Valley on another tech start-up but after my first daughter was born, looked for a more stable, larger company to work with. In 2002, I joined W.R. Grace back in Boston, in their mergers and acquisitions effort, which gave me the opportunity to travel the world in search of deals. Through 11 years with Grace, I held leadership positions in both marketing and general management. From 2007 to 2010, I ran the North Asia P&L for Grace's construction business based out of Tokyo. After returning, I was promoted to Vice President of Marketing for their Performance Chemical Division.

I'm currently the Vice President of Marketing at the Swagelok Company, reporting to its CEO Art Anton. Swagelok is a $1.8

billion, privately held company headquartered in Solon, Ohio. In my current role, my team is responsible for strategy development and acquisitions, product and market management, pricing and business analytics, key account management, and field services. I have over 70 direct and nearly 200 indirect reports. My joint degree background helps me with my international relationships, and many globally appreciate my breadth of interests.

My wife, Julie, is Korean American, and we have two daughters, Rachel and Emily. We enjoy helping with Asian causes and have a yen for Asian food.

The joint degree program changed my life and enabled me to be different from other MBAs. I would strongly encourage others with similar interests to take that road less traveled; it will not be linear, but it will be exciting and rewarding.

MARTHA MASTERMAN GORDON—CSEAS 1999

I grew up in a small lumber town in Eastern Oregon, where the 12,000 residents loved their little town for its quiet streets, strong sense of community, and connection to the expansive mountains, snaking rivers, and lush valleys that mark this unique part of the Pacific Northwest. Although the area was a great place to grow up, after graduating, I wanted to branch out and explore the "big city" of Portland and other more diverse university towns of the west side of the state. So, to Lewis & Clark College I went and found my niche through studies of international affairs. I was drawn to this field of study as it gave me an outlet to explore far-reaching ideas and places, from how countries and institutions operate at a macro level to a deep dive into an area of fascination for me—Southeast Asia.

At the time, my reasons to focus on that region were twofold: first, this burgeoning area in the early 1990s was hot—as the economic growth engine of Asia, the Four Tigers (Hong Kong, Singapore, South Korea, and Taiwan) and their neighboring countries created energy and excitement. The rapid modernization of their industries and their integration into a global economy was timely, fun, and interesting to study. Pragmatically, I felt having expertise in this region could be valuable. Second, the culture, people, and geography of the region fascinated me—they held a beauty and mystique that I wanted to understand more. It was the perfect complement of practical and creative, hard and soft.

I should mention too that while growing up in La Grande, my mother had a hand in broadening our minds outside of the rather homogenous community we lived in. She was the local chapter president of AFS (American Field Service), a global exchange student program. Students from other countries were a regular appearance in our home, and we hosted a student from Indonesia for a year. This played no small part, I imagine, in fueling my interest to expand my horizons beyond our small town and was my first real introduction to Southeast Asia.

After Lewis & Clark, I yearned to spend time "on the ground" in Southeast Asia so spent a year (through connections with our former exchange student) teaching English as a second language at Satya Wacana Christian University, a private university in Salatiga, Indonesia. Though a year was barely enough time to scratch the surface of this vast archipelago, I was ready to begin a graduate program and get my career more formally on track. I knew that more study of Southeast Asia would be my focus, so the University of Michigan was a natural fit. My older brother, Andrew Masterman, had completed a joint degree MBA/MA in Asian Studies, and his experience was all the research I needed. I was considering pairing this degree with either business or public policy (again, my practical side coming through), and under the guidance of Professor Linda Lim, I was convinced that business would be a choice that would allow for a broader range of opportunities down the road.

My experience in the joint degree program at U of M was tremendous. In one day, I would flip from studying Indonesian language or anthropology to calculating net present value in finance. It tested my abilities and expanded my thinking in ways I hadn't anticipated. The business school provided me with focus for my career, as I naturally gravitated to studies of consumer behavior and marketing. The Southeast Asian studies coursework expanded my understanding of the history, politics, language, and culture that shape this region. The two disciplines intersected in Linda Lim's courses, as well as when I wrote my thesis on the coffee industry in Southeast Asia. In this research, I explored ways that the developed world and Southeast Asian small coffee farmers might connect in a mutually beneficial way and, in particular, methods for the farmers to gain a more equitable share through the value chain.

With a marketing focus, my career started at the Campbell Soup Company, where I was able to build a foundation in classical brand management. After four years there, followed by a move back to Michigan (for my husband's engineering career) and two children, I transitioned into a consulting career in which I worked with large consumer packaged goods (CPG) firms on their innovation and brand strategy. I continued that work at both small (Arbor Strategy Group) and large (GfK) firms and now do this type of work as a freelance consultant. The majority of my work is domestic, although I have had a handful of global projects. My life and work took me on a path that did not lead to Asia, as that perhaps took a back seat to family and developing a marketing and consulting career here in the United States.

I have been able to tap back into my interest in Asia through volunteer work as a board member for Ten Thousand Villages, a national fair trade retailer that improves the lives of makers by supporting their businesses and providing a fair, stable income. Improving the lives of others through connecting our developed market to Southeast Asia has always been a central driver of my interest in the region, and in this role I'm able to link my marketing and business skills to that more socially oriented goal.

Although my career has not gone the Asia route, I believe the joint degree MBA/MA in Asian Studies made me a more well-rounded, open-minded, and strategic thinker. It provided a way for me to concurrently explore my liberal arts side and transition into a business career, which wasn't immediately a natural fit for me. The joint degree and experience of living in the region helped shape me into what I am today. I am very thankful for taking that leap at a young age, and I would encourage any student to expand their horizons through study and/or work abroad.

JOEL SAMUELS—CCS 2001

Although I never got a job in a China-related field, I think I benefited from the experience of going through the joint degree program. I was exposed to some great professors and important thinkers, learned a difficult foreign language, and expanded the way I look at a lot of things.

If there was a weaker portion of the experience, I'd have to say it was the school of business. I was never able to see how the classes in the MBA track made a real difference in anyone's ability to think or do things. If anything, I saw it as a two-year "credentialing" process so that after graduation, most people could re-enter their careers in a job similar to the one they had before but just at a much higher salary.

I've found a different niche, and I am pleased to say that there are times when my business education comes into play. I learned enough about business at U of M and in law school to become the first prosecutor in California to present a criminal case to a grand jury that resulted in an indictment of a corporation for murder. Unfortunately, I wasn't able to obtain a criminal conviction, but the case did settle for an injunction that forced oversight over the company's business practices and substantial fines.

I think the program was ahead of its time when I was in it in the late 1980s. At that time, the idea of educating people to be involved in U.S.-China trade was not well developed or accepted. What happened at Tiananmen in 1989 was certainly a blow as well. I think you and the others who were a part of the great upward arc of trade, business, and social relations between the United States and China should be rightfully proud of your foresight and efforts.

Of course, who knows where things will go from here? Maybe my kids and yours and the kids of the other graduates of the program will have something to do with that. It will be interesting to see.

JON BLUMENAUER—CSEAS 2002

My childhood growing up in Portland, Oregon, made me a pretty unlikely candidate for a life in Asia. Basketball was my first love, and baseball wasn't too far behind. After playing both at Pomona College in California, I was unable to fathom a professional career that didn't in some way connect to sports. Shortly after graduation, I was fortunate to join Nike at the company's world headquarters outside Portland, which seemed like a perfect fit. During my initial interview with Nike, I was told that one possible path was in apparel manufacturing. And while there were no guarantees, if I was hired and things went well, there may be an opportunity to move to Asia. For a young kid who had only been out of the country once on a summer trip to Europe, this possibility was alluring, if a little scary.

Fast-forward 22 months: I was living in Singapore, managing Nike contract factories there and in Malaysia and Sri Lanka. I had never been to Asia, I spoke no Asian language, and my only preparation was to be given a copy of a book called *The Overseas Handbook*, which was so general it could have applied to the post I left in North Carolina.

But I was immediately fascinated by the region. Everything was new and exciting. Everything was different. It made me both appreciate both where I came from and the new cultures I was immersed in. Over the next seven plus years, I moved to Thailand then to Viet Nam—the geographic equivalent of going from Los Angeles to Portland to Boise. But the complexity in that small area was incredible; different cultures, religions, political structures, languages, food, and ways of doing business meant that every day was a challenge and a learning experience. Outside of work, I traveled for fun. And the more remote the location, the more exciting and enchanting the experience.

My sense of curiosity, adventure, and needing to be in constant learning mode never waned. I often thought to myself, "Eventually this will subside. Eventually it will all become 'normal.'" But it never did. If anything, my curiosity—along with my attachment to the region—grew. After nine years with Nike, working in five different locations and four different countries, I wanted to set myself up for the next step in my career by going to business school. But I knew I wanted to return to Asia after my studies and to stay connected to the region during them.

The opportunity to do this through the Southeast Asian Studies program made U of M the obvious choice. There I would be able to augment the practical knowledge I gained living in Asia with more formal study of history and languages. And after living in tropical climates for so long, what better place to keep me inside focused on my studies than blood-thickening Michigan? There I was able to get great instruction and make fantastic friends who shared my connection and love for the region. Being able to mix classes between programs allowed me to balance the content in a way that made the material in each more interesting. It also allowed me to broaden my circle of friends and professors.

One of the big draws to the Southeast Asian Studies program was the opportunity for high-level language study. I was very fortunate to study Thai for five semesters and Bahasa Indonesian for two semesters in a very intensive format. I spent both of my summers between school years in Thailand—the first studying Thai, the second at an internship with Johnson & Johnson—which kept me connected and my language skills improving. Although I am far from fluent, the skills I developed allowed me to have great adventures and develop friendships that would never have been possible otherwise.

After graduation, I was able to connive my way into a job in Indonesia, this time working for an Indonesian apparel and sports equipment manufacturer. The company was owned by a Chinese Indonesian and staffed with Korean and Chinese Indonesian managers. I was the only *bule*, or Westerner, in the company. This was another incredible—if challenging—experience navigating new cultures and testing the limits of my language ability. Since I couldn't speak Korean, and the Koreans couldn't speak English, we communicated in Bahasa Indonesian, which made for some interesting meetings. Later it was back to Thailand to work with a former Nike colleague, then a move to Europe before coming back home to Portland in 2006, where I still live and work at the furniture manufacturing company that I took over in 2013.

Although I'm back "home," I'm still trying to figure out how to move back to Asia, because my heart is still truly there. I had too many adventures to count with great friends, and what made it special were the people whom I met along the way. Some are still good friends to this day; others—from encounters that took place in remote villages; on bus, train, boat, or scooter rides; or when invited into someone's home for tea—will never remember me, but I will never forget them. The language training made these encounters a bit deeper and more meaningful; the areas studies added powerful context. And the connections with people were incredible. The warmth, kindness, and curiosity exhibited to a stranger who clearly was very different is something that touched me and provides a very stark contrast with how things are in the United States right now.

Since moving back to Portland, I continue to remember my Asia days fondly, to connect with friends on frequent trips back (although they are a little less frequent now with a couple small kids). I appreciate the opportunities the program gave me to get to know and learn from really sharp people and to deepen my connection to a part of the world that I truly love.

MARK GUTHRIE—CSEAS 2002

I grew up in Terre Haute, Indiana. My father was a professor of analytical chemistry at Rose-Hulman Institute of Technology. My mother was an elementary school teacher who later (after raising four boys) worked in the library at Indiana State University. Among my other early interests, I was very active in the Boy Scouts and worked eight summers as a camp counselor. Perhaps because of this experience, I ended up studying civil and environmental engineering at Duke University and later earned an MSCE in Environmental Engineering from Purdue University.

After leaving Purdue, I worked for seven years as a consulting engineer in Atlanta, Georgia, specializing in industrial waste management and treatment process engineering. During that time, I had two short overseas assignments in Japan and Korea, which I thoroughly enjoyed. It was therefore an easy decision to accept a staff position in our international division, based in Bangkok, Thailand, with responsibility for both marketing and execution of projects involving industrial and hazardous waste management in Asia. Over time I also became involved in planning, design, and management of water, wastewater, and other municipal environmental infrastructure projects.

During my first 10 years overseas, I worked on projects for industries, local and national governments, and international assistance agencies in nearly every country within Asia and the Arabian Gulf region. Eventually I became less of a technical specialist and more of a general problem solver, providing inputs on a wide variety of environmental projects in different countries and cultures. However, I still felt that I lacked some key management skills required to successfully meet future career challenges—and to have a greater influence over critical decisions in the project development cycle.

I was also ready for a change and felt a need to spend some time in the United States. However, I knew that I wanted to continue my career path in Asia. In looking at different MBA programs, I was impressed with what the University of Michigan had to offer. Not only would I be able to acquire the management tools I sought, I would also be able to pursue interests in Asian history, culture, and languages through the MBA/MA in Asian Studies dual degree program.

Having spent more time in Thailand than anywhere else, I opted for the Southeast Asian program and continued my study of the Thai language, including the summer Advanced Study of Thai Program at Chiang Mai University. I also took Indonesian during my third year in the program. As well as improving my language skills, I especially enjoyed the Southeast Asian history courses taught by Victor Lieberman and John Whitmore and a course on Burmese Buddhism taught by Patrick Pranke. I also liked the weekly "brown bag" seminars organized by the Center for Southeast Asian Studies, as they brought together an amazing variety of people from different disciplines throughout the university, all sharing an interest in the Southeast Asia region.

On the MBA side, I admire and appreciate the efforts of Linda Lim and Gunter Dufey—both as teachers, and mentors—who did so much to advance the Asian Studies programs at Michigan. I only regret that I arrived too late to take any courses from Pete Gosling, but I treasure the opportunities I had to talk with him at the many social gatherings he and Linda hosted at their home.

My path to attending Michigan was perhaps a bit unusual, and at 41 years of age, it came later in life than for most MBA and MA students. I joke that it was my alternative to a more traditional mid-life crisis, but in truth I would do it all over again. My career path was not much changed after Michigan, as I continued to do environment-related work, but I was able to perform in different roles that included economic and financial feasibility analysis of infrastructure projects and design and implementation of institutional strengthening programs. I have also done some corporate financial advisory work with a friend who went through the same MBA/MA program about 10 years before me. Today, I continue to take on occasional consulting assignments but am otherwise retired and enjoying my friends and golfing in Thailand.

NEIL HARRISON—CJS 2005

"Why Japan?" I have fielded that question innumerable times, and it's always a long, somewhat rambling answer. I guess it's a combination of things. For one, my father had a large Japanese company as a client, and I always took interest in what he shared about Japanese business culture. I was also a young adventurous eater and have vivid memories of my first tastes of miso soup, sushi, tempura, etc. But, if I am being honest, I also think it's because I was a bit bored of numerous years of Spanish language classes. Japanese was offered my senior year in high school, and I jumped at the chance to take it. I immediately enjoyed the challenge of learning the language, but I also thoroughly enjoyed the cultural lessons that accompanied my early study of Japanese grammar, hiragana, katakana, and kanji. In short, I was hooked early.

When I started classes as a freshman at the University of Pennsylvania, I selected Japanese at least in part to satisfy the foreign language requirement. However, two instructors in particular, Yukako Ommura and Tomoko Takami, were both unbelievable and had a significant impact on my continued (and increasing) interest in all things Japan. Both were so kind and clearly passionate about teaching but strict and disciplined when they needed to be (as most Japanese language instructors are) to ensure that students were putting in their best effort. I loved the intensive regimen—classes every day, pop quizzes, challenging tests every Friday—and I also loved learning more about Japanese culture, customs, history, etc.

I soon added a number of Japan-related courses to my curriculum and eventually decided to dual major in International

Relations and Asian and Middle Eastern Studies. I continued with daily Japanese language classes all the way through senior year and counted courses in Japanese history and culture, Chinese civilization, and a political science course about Asia as my favorites. I spent two summers interning at the Japanese Chamber of Commerce and Industry in New York and started to think more about doing something related to Japan for my career. Given its relevance today, it's worth mentioning that my senior thesis was written in reaction to North Korea's 1998 test firing of a missile over Japan into the Pacific Ocean. At that time, this was a shocking development as it demonstrated North Korea's advancing technological capabilities. As a result, I decided to write about U.S.-Japan relations and the implications of missile defense deployment in Asia.

My career aspirations took a bit of a turn in the summer of my junior year. I applied to a number of Japan-related internships, including an opportunity at Price Waterhouse's Japanese business group. Despite a lack of any real technical acumen, my résumé was forwarded to a small business unit called the Advanced Software Engineering Center. To this day, I am not sure how I landed that internship, but I had a great experience, learned a tremendous amount, and started to develop a similar, passionate interest in technology. That interest became strong enough that I joined a small management consultancy called Diamond Technology Partners upon graduation as I was attracted by the prospect of assisting large companies with exploiting opportunities being created by the "dot-com bubble" and all manner of digital disruption.

Fast-forward a few years, and I started to think more and more about attending business school. I missed being a student and was excited at the prospect of being back on a university campus. I also knew that I was probably only getting one more chance to go back to school. I definitely wanted to advance my career, but I also wanted to focus my education on topics in which I had a deep interest—including Asia and Japan. Thus, I started to look at programs that would allow me adequate time to focus on topics outside of the typical business school curriculum. I looked at several programs but quickly turned my eye toward Michigan. I knew Ann Arbor would be a fun place to spend some time as my twin sister and a few friends had attended Michigan for college, and I had visited them several times. I also knew that I would have access to a great business education as well as other tremendous educational opportunities across the university.

That certainly turned out to be true as I encountered high-quality Japanese language instructors and top-notch professors for truly great courses. Particularly memorable experiences included Japanese law with Professor Mark West (head of the Center for Japanese Studies at the time and now Dean of Michigan's Law School), Japanese cinema with Professor Markus Nornes, an urban planning course about the impact of globalization on Asian megacities with Gavin Shatkin, and a course in the College of Engineering about lean manufacturing and the Toyota production system. I also had the experience of a lifetime participating in a summer cultural immersion program on the outskirts of Kyoto. I stayed with a Japanese family and had a long but enjoyable daily commute—by train and bicycle—to the campus of the Japan Center for Michigan Universities on the shores of Lake Biwa. I still have a vivid picture in my mind of windsurfers practicing on the lake just outside the window of the classroom. Simply amazing, as were my other adventures throughout Japan that summer.

Back at the business school (re-named from Michigan Business School to the Ross School of Business during my tenure), I also had a great all-around experience with impressive classmates who were also navigating the two-year whirlwind that is business school: intensive classes, countless group projects, and numerous extra-curricular activities, not to mention school-wide and section happy hours and social events and my fair share of Michigan football, basketball, and hockey games. My wife, Wendy, and I thoroughly enjoyed all aspects of our Michigan experience and always look forward to opportunities to come back to Ann Arbor.

I would be remiss in closing without mentioning the influence of Professor Linda Lim on so many students at Michigan. Professor Lim was the Asia expert in the business school during my time there and the primary link between the business school and the university's Asian centers (e.g., Center for Japanese Studies, Center for Southeast Asian Studies, etc.). She taught a popular MBA course on Business in Asia that I loved, not just because of my interest in the topic but also because of Professor Lim's ability to foster an amazing classroom environment—an environment in which she almost literally pulled the Asian students in the class into the conversation. This provided for a lively and entertaining discussion about business in China, Japan, Thailand, Singapore, Indonesia, and other countries, highlighted by firsthand accounts from my classmates who were from those countries. I listened intently, took a lot of notes, and enjoyed every minute. Professor Lim was also the faculty sponsor for (and general force behind) the annual, long-running Asian Business Conference (ABC), which attracted impressive guest speakers from the worlds of politics and business to create a great opportunity for students to discuss a range of relevant topics.

I will always look back on my time at Michigan fondly. It was a simply a great experience from an educational, professional, and personal perspective. Of course, the best part of graduating from Michigan is that I am now part of Michigan's incomparable network of passionate alumni, including classmates from around the world who have become business contacts and, more importantly, great friends.

CHAPTER 4.

ALUMNI ESSAYS ON BUSINESS IN ASIA

EXPATRIATE MODELS IN ASIA—PAST, PRESENT, AND FUTURE

By Michael Little, MBA/MA China, 1994

Who takes the journey to work in faraway places? Is it an expert, adaptable to all things strange and different, speaking foreign languages, who chooses to leave home and travel far? Or is the reality more of expatriate compounds in the Middle East recreating suburban America or the inside of an Irish pub on the 15th floor of a skyscraper in Hong Kong?

This collection is full of people who had a passion for things different and far away, who were educated as experts in cultures and peoples far away. But when we look at expatriate communities today, "Our Man in Paris" has disappeared. The expatriate who knows the local people, speaks the local language, and can explain local customs has been supplanted by families on three-year assignments or individuals attracted by the money of the expat "bubble" lifestyle. So has T. E. Lawrence been replaced by John Doe of Akron, Ohio, with a family of three, cost of living adjustment, housing allowance, and home leave business class return? Here is my quick overview.

Distance and Following Local Customs Are an Impediment to Trust

The East India Company (EIC) had its share of expatriate stories. One of my favorites is in William Dalrymple's *White Mughals* (London: Penguin, 2002, p. 481), where the EIC resident in Hyderabad was their man in the subcontinent, well versed in local language and customs. However, he managed to amass a fortune of £85,000 by 1820 apparently by taking advantage of his position (soliciting bribes is the unsubstantiated accusation) and being many months removed away from the board of directors in London. He resigned in advance of receiving a letter from the EIC board removing him from his office.

Socialization Around Company Norms and Centralized Human Resources

The History of the Hongkong and Shanghai Banking Corporation by Frank H. H. King (Cambridge: Cambridge University Press, 1988, four volumes) gives an insight into 19th- and early 20th-century expatriate recruiting. A young employee would join a management program and work for several years with more seasoned staff in the head office to learn the company culture and the business. Sounds very modern. In the case of HSBC, the London office was the starting point. P. G. Wodehouse made the initial cut but later decided that banking was not for him. Then once the young staff were considered ready, they would join a regional office in Hong Kong or Bombay to further learn the business before being sent to manage a branch on their own. The successful management of a branch for a number of years would lead either to a country level responsibility or a return to the regional or global level.

A Hierarchy Segregated by Role: Executive, Management, and Labor

Of course, the drawback was there were never much more than a hundred "Eastern staff," and in the world before 1950, they were all white males. They were a small group who all knew one another from the same schools, clubs, and afternoon sports. And they were of "one corporate culture." But the staff were racially segregated. The white Eastern staff comprised the upper and middle management. Lower management, the clerks and tellers, were referred to as the "Portuguese" and were typically mixed-race. At the bottom were the local staff, often managed via a comprador.

Often the Hierarchy Is Racially Based

My first experience with expatriates was very similar to the HSBC model. A small group of white males—Americans in an inner circle with a few British, Australians, and New Zealanders surrounding them—made up the modern Eastern staff. The next layer was composed of Malaysians, Singaporeans, and Hong Kong Chinese with Western education, or the "Portuguese." And at the bottom, the local business partners, capitalist or communist, effectively controlled the local staff in place of the compradors who died out in the 1950s. The only positive is that in the 1990s movement between the groups was at least contemplated if not common.

The Japanese take this model in a new direction. The roles of both the Eastern staff and the "Portuguese" (senior and middle management positions) are filled by Japanese or extremely well socialized non-Japanese. The middle management roles are paired, one Japanese and one local, to facilitate communication and control of the local staff and to socialize local management trainees.

Expatriate Experiences as a Path to Success at Home and Less Incentive to Learn about the Locals

But there has been a significant change in the past 20 years. In the EIC and HSBC, even up into the 1990s, the senior Eastern staff were lifelong expatriates. They chose to stay overseas, moving from country to country, job to job. Now the expatriate assignment is seen as a prerequisite to a senior management role, a ticket to be punched. So executives pack up their families and move abroad for shorter stays, sometimes as little as 13 months, to get the stamp of expatriate.

On the positive side, this reinforces the core company culture through the movement of the leaders around the world and the export of practices and standards. The negative impact is the short-term nature of the assignments and the short-term outlook of the executives. For the executives, the imperative becomes to get through 36 months without any blemish and return home. For the local staff, directives from above that are not well received are simply met with passive "waiting it out" strategies as every expatriate has a clock ticking over their head. And needless to say, executives with a full-time job find it easier to hire local staff acculturated to foreigners than to learn local languages and customs.

More Expatriates Than Ever, Just Spending Less Time Overseas

The increase in air travel has radically altered the nature of the expatriate assignment. In the 1970s, a flight from Paris to Singapore was a long affair with stops in the Middle East and Sri Lanka before reaching the destination. Today almost any two major cities are connected directly; home is a direct flight away.

Aligning the Local Staff to Company Goals Is a Challenge If You Don't Understand the Local Staff

The "Portuguese" have all but disappeared. The mixed-race or third-country middle management have been pushed out by local staff. Similarly, the compradors have disappeared as foreign firms found more educated locals available to hire. These middle managers were a fulcrum in many ways, carrying the local knowledge of "how things are done," facilitating communication between the executives and local staff, and being directly aligned with the goals of the foreign company. Local staff are often caught in the middle, intentionally or unintentionally, between foreign companies and local politics.

My favorite Asian management fable is about an operation in

Southeast Asia. The American-educated management team were all local but were never considered for regional or global jobs. The regional senior managers in Hong Kong were all American and European expatriates. The local management team decided to cook the books and maximize their bonuses, which they did for a number of years. When the company accounts ran dry, the money having been paid out for performance that had not occurred, the local team called up the regional headquarters, confessed, resigned, and then said: "Don't bother suing, we went to school with the Chief Justice of the Supreme Court."

Failure to supervise, failure to understand the other, and ultimately failure to develop the other. You cannot say all people are equal and then treat them differently without teaching them a double standard.

Is the Short-Term Expatriate Assignment Worth It to the Employee and the Company?

Then why don't companies want the long-term expatriates? When I first worked overseas, the executives would often shut down conversations with comments like, "We tried that ten years ago, what has changed? Nothing." Today the executives do not have that long-term memory available to them. But what caused the real demise of the long-term expatriates?

Cost surely plays a part as the expenses of expatriates and their families have skyrocketed. The average middle manager expatriate in Shanghai takes home USD 272,000/year or almost twice as much as they would receive at home (http://www.forbes.com/sites/jnylander/2015/05/20/expat-pay-is-getting-fatter-in-china/#254897916254). As the expatriate model has shifted from a lifelong choice to a short-term assignment, the thinking has been that the expatriate must be compensated for the inconvenience and cost of living. Thus salaries, benefits, and corporate ranks are used as rewards for expatriate assignments.

They Become a Caste That Serves Only Themselves

The other reason for the decline of long-term expatriates is that they reorganize their business world to suit themselves. Left on their own, as in the management fable above, the incentive is to make the business opaque. Without scrutiny, the expatriates become a self-perpetuating class, interested in only their own survival and perks.

Expatriate Jobs Are Too Critical to Trust to the Expatriates

Why not then cultural experts? Why not people who know their home corporate culture and the local culture and can be that fulcrum between the two?

Returning to the East India Company example, even 200 years ago there was a great concern that individuals if left on their own would drift into "native habits" and come to act differently and even sympathize with locals. Hence that letter to Hyderabad firing the resident. Distance breeds mistrust and difference breeds fear. An education in another culture teaches questioning of assumptions both in the home and foreign cultures. The HSBC model, and by extension the other models, are all command and control. That is the key to their success. I think this is often why you find ex-military personnel in expatriate roles, the unquestioning following of orders.

Ken Lieberthal summed it up in a talk I attended. "The China business," he said, "is so important companies send the best and brightest to run it. But then it is so important they manage the business down a telephone line."

The irony of course is the current management fad for enhanced speed in decision making in business and unleashing the potential of the organization through empowering managers. None of that works in the current expatriate context. It is a recipe for failure. The local staff are not to be trusted or ready, and the expatriate staff are commanded and controlled. While the ideal would be for companies to leverage cultural knowledge, direction from the center feels safer. But it cannot last.

~ ~ ~

THE HERMIT CRAB DILEMMA: CHALLENGES FACING JAPANESE COMPANIES IN A STAGNANT ECONOMY

By Arif Iqball, MBA/MA Japan, 1995

Two decades ago, Japan was basking in the sun, and prospects for growth were never brighter with growing innovative exports and Western companies feverishly adopting Japanese management styles. Today, Japanese companies are in a very different situation, paralyzed by an aging demographic, a receding economic environment, and limitations created by the Japanese management culture. Whatever happened to Japan and Japanese innovation, and is there a way to come out of the crisis?

Even before my first visit to Japan in 1993, I had been impressed by Japanese "innovation." After all, Japan had brought us the bullet train, the pocket calculator, the Walkman, the laptop computer, and recently, emoji. As I spent more time in Japan, I started to notice that innovation in Japan did not necessarily target financial rewards but necessity and customer experience. Take for example one of the biggest innovations that I always miss when I am not in Japan (especially in winter)—the wonderful and civilized experience of using the Japanese toilet seat.

For the uninitiated, although it looks like a Western toilet at first glance, the Japanese toilet has numerous additional features included either in part of the toilet or in the seat—ranging from a blow dryer, seat heating, massage options, water jet and temperature adjustments, automatic lid opening, automatic flushing, blood pressure monitoring, protein count, and the ability to control room heating and air conditioning. Many toilet seats allow you to play your own MP3 music. Modest Japanese women uncomfortable with the sound of bodily functions when using the toilet would flush over and over again, wasting a lot of water, so there is a function that simulates the sound of flushing, thus saving real water.

You see, the Japanese realized that the average person spends 1.5 years of their total life on the toilet seat so felt it was worthwhile to create a good user experience. They really had thought through the whole value chain and continue to innovate. For example, recently, as an experiment, Narita airport has installed special toilet paper for sanitizing your smartphone.

Not only is this type of innovation the norm, but it is also encouraged in both government and business. For example, Japan has a Toilet of the Year award given by the Ministry of Land, Infrastructure, and Transportation. Avon Japan gave its prestigious Woman of the Year award to a designer of toilets who leveraged public toilet design to improve community communication (e.g., one of the projects was to improve communication space via bathroom design for schoolgirls in a school where bullying existed).

But why are such examples of Japanese innovation and success becoming less frequent? What is happening to Japan and Japanese innovation lately? The short answer is that innovation still happens, but the speed and focus are now limited by a combination of factors: demographics, economy, and Japanese management culture.

Japan has the oldest population in the world, so risk-taking is not a priority, and since these older people also have higher savings and strong purchase power, recent innovation is catered toward them—for instance, fax machines are still in regular use across Japan. This aging demographic has also influenced Japanese management culture.

As the economy grew in the 1970s, 1980s, and early 1990s, people became less hungry for growth. The affluent 1980s and 1990s were still impacted by a generation of people who were overachievers, many of them driven by their strong sense of pride to prove their self-worth in postwar Japan. More recently, two decades of recession have had a strong impact on available capital, and companies now have limited funds and resources for seeds and experimentation.

It is ironic how the once strong Japanese management culture and the fundamental pillars of that culture and style, such as lifetime employment, seniority-based promotions, etc., are now responsible for the downward spiral of innovation in Japanese companies.

Lifetime employment, introduced at one time as a retention tool, is a prominent factor in reduced risk-taking by employees and even management, with the focus on not rocking the status quo (especially in turbulent economic times). The role of senior management is primarily one of a consensus builder versus being a champion of change, since failure usually marks the end of a career due to loss of goodwill and trust.

The seniority-based and regular/similar bonus system initiated to avoid jealousy also eliminates any need to shine. Limited career tracks and salaries for scientists and technical staff have discouraged new talent and encouraged existing talent to change departments.

In typical Japanese companies now, unlike in other countries, invention comes from in-house resources (vs. collaboration or, as in the past, via government sponsored consortiums). To avoid big changes that may confuse the customers, it is a culture of Kaizen (continuous improvement) versus innovation, and unless all aspects of the idea have been satisfactorily tested, it does not get the go-ahead or ongoing support from wary sales staff.

A historically inward focus limits Japanese companies to focus on Japanese customers only. They really did not care about the rest of the world since previously all profits were made at home versus products sold overseas, whose pricing was adjusted to gain market share. While that profit sanctuary approach worked earlier, the changing Japanese market situation (primarily increased competition at home from foreign companies and impact of recession) now requires Japanese companies to go global to have a sufficient revenue base and profitability to survive.

The Hermit Crab Dilemma

Hermit crabs are small crustaceans with a soft underbody that they protect by carrying a shell on their back. The shell of the hermit crab is not its own but one that belonged to another animal, such as a snail, periwinkle, or oyster drill. Their soft, coiled abdomen fits tightly inside the "borrowed" shell. As it ages, the hermit crab outgrows its borrowed shell and is thus faced with the dilemma of either starving itself to remain in the existing shell or finding a new shell.

Recently many Japanese companies are in a similar dilemma as the hermit crab, but the choice and/or action is not that easy due to aging demographics, with employees and often management preferring no change as they gradually phase out via retirement. Transformative companies do exist but are the exception and not the norm.

Recently, companies like Rakuten and Uniqlo have taken bold steps to change their management culture even to the point of making English language compulsory at all levels of communication. Recent demographic and economic trends have encouraged mid-level hiring, and Western-style mobility across companies has picked up. There has also been movement in hiring at the senior management and board of directors level in companies like Takeda and Shiseido.

Although transformative actions were taken by a few Japanese companies in the past, these were not strategic or systematic enough but rather opportunistic—hence the results were not sustainable. But recent M&A efforts by the likes of Softbank, Uniqlo, and Rakuten are highly strategic in nature and effectively leverage these mergers and acquisitions to improve innovation.

Innovation at Foreign Companies and Start-Ups

Innovation in many areas now comes from outside Japan, and

more interesting to watch are foreign companies and start-ups. When I first moved to Japan, I would always hear that Japanese customers are "unique," but over time, they are becoming more and more like the rest of the world. At the advertising agency McCann, with its broad Japanese and non-Japanese company customer base, I could see that what the Japanese consumers really wanted were "value" products—desired attributes at a reasonable price. This "value" concept has worked well for innovative foreign companies like Amazon, Ikea, Costco, Seiyu (Walmart), H&M, etc., notably companies that are in control of their product distribution and able to bring global innovation to Japanese customers at affordable prices. These companies have grown at a relatively fast rate compared to other Japanese companies during the same time period.

Venture capital funding in Japan is growing, and more young Japanese are approaching the start-up world. The app market in Japan is ahead of that in the United States in terms of adoption and innovation, but it is not at the same volume or scale as in the United States, the key difference being that these entrepreneurs are visionary on a small scale but not aggressive or hungry enough to want to change Japan.

Under Prime Minister Abe, the Japanese government is also trying to encourage start-ups and find new areas of innovation and growth (e.g., military-related opportunities in aircraft and submarine manufacturing are now available for high-quality Japanese manufacturing), with the hope that Japan will innovate here based on its past experience and manufacturing excellence strengths.

Case Study of Innovation in a Japanese Company—Benesse Corporation

The Benesse Group, listed on the Tokyo Stock Exchange as Benesse Holdings, Inc., provides a variety of services that include correspondence courses, support for schools, cram and prep schools, language training, and overseas study to realize the new type of education that develops the capabilities needed by

Japanese society in the future. Benesse Corporation, a group company, is the largest Japanese correspondence education company but is facing decline in revenue recently due to lower birth rates and the emergence of many competitors who have copied or adapted its model.

Benesse over the last few years has tried to globalize itself and simultaneously revolutionize education in Japan, which could only have been tried by a company of Benesse's scale and scope. The many actions taken were aimed at innovating not only at the product level but also at the business model level. The company

- hired a new experienced CEO (a Japanese celebrity as a professional executive);
- hired a new management team with significant global experience;
- hired a non-Japanese CFO to implement Western-style finance (involving business consulting versus the Japanese style accounting-only focus);
- invested in use of technology and analytics to shift the education paradigm (using a bring your own device such as an iPad to allow customized tutoring);
- established an "Ed Tech" office in Silicon Valley to bring education best practices to Japan;
- launched several joint ventures and collaborations (Udemy, Softbank, Bic Camera, Apple, etc.) to improve content, capacity, and supply capability;
- created "buzz" via countrywide "touch and try" locations;
- incentivized management to meet their "full potential"; and
- self-financed significant growth initiatives.

Early Lessons Learned

- The globalization story did not excite many staff and senior management who felt threatened about their future.

- The sense of urgency and openness to outsiders was disguised well with *Honne/Tatemae* (true thoughts versus publicly displayed thoughts).

- The company misread the market's desire to adapt/accept the new innovative company direction.

- The company misread parents' continued social preference for cram- school–style teaching.

- Western-style "bad news first" did not work as critical information from the front line was lost in organizational hierarchy.

- The company misread board of directors' tolerance and time line for risk-taking on new approaches.

Some Suggestions

Starting a positive innovation domino at Japanese companies requires a fundamental shift in changing the corporate culture in traditional Japanese companies while handling demographic and economic challenges.

- It all starts with people, and unfortunately due to the aging demographics and decreasing birth rate, there is a limited domestic pool of qualified people to choose from. Increasing English skills would open up a world of higher-quality talent. The government has taken positive steps here by reducing the requirements for permanent residency for qualified foreign nationals.

- Hold HR accountable for talent strategy and development.

- Eliminate blockers: enforce an "up or out" policy for middle management.

- Japanese management does not want to be a bearer of bad news and wants to protect personal relationships. Teach management about having "difficult conversations" that are also important for wins in global negotiations.

- Establish new reward mechanisms for outstanding individuals and/or group contributions to invention and innovation.

- Incentivize innovation and risk-taking especially at the senior management level, for example, Silicon Valley noble failures list.

- Actively reallocate capital and resources from non-strategic projects/businesses to self-fund growth.

- Increase M&A not just for revenue increase but for integration of innovation and best practices.

- Increase joint ventures with local companies and especially overseas to overcome cost, scale, and inexperience.

- Mandate boards of directors to push for innovation, appointing a BOD Innovation Committee to challenge innovation and achievement of full potential results.

A Story of Two Fish

This is a story of two fish usually found swimming in the deep depths of the dark ocean. One day the adventurous younger fish lost its way and swam out of the water, into the air, and then back into the water. Excited at the realization of the difference between water and air, the younger fish went back and asked the older fish, "Do you know that we live in water and there is air above the water?" The older fish having never seen air denies the fact that air can even exist or that they live in water. The younger fish challenges and leads the older fish out of the water and then back into the water, and now they both recognize the difference between water and air and the fact that they live in water.

Sometimes leaders in an organization have to raise awareness and take both types of fish out of the water and then back into the water to make them aware of their current state. It takes very strong leadership to change the current Japanese culture. Sometimes the fish will refuse to swim with the leader. This refusal can be overcome at the staff level, but what if the senior management refuses to come along?

The companies who find a way to overcome their own cultural barriers will innovate and succeed in the future. As the saying goes, "Sometimes you just have to jump from the stage of the Kiyomizu-dera temple and let the gods carry you."

Let's hope there are many. My retirement depends on them.

CHAPTER 5.

ALUMNI BIOGRAPHIES

MBA/MA IN ASIAN STUDIES (CENTER FOR CHINESE STUDIES)

Jeffrey BISTRONG received a BA degree in Government from Colby College and the MBA/ MA in Asian Studies from U-M (1988) and also studied politics at the University of York. His banking career spans almost three decades at BancBoston Robertson Stephens and Harris Williams & Co., where he founded and heads the Technology, Media & Telecom Group. Jeff has led M&A advisory assignments for software, SaaS, IT services, internet, digital media, telecommunications, and technology hardware companies, and in verticals including healthcare IT, financial technology, energy and power, transportation & logistics, and not-for-profit. He has extensive cross-border transaction experience in Latin America, Europe, and Asia and has been a member of many corporate boards. Jeff lives in Manchester-by-the-Sea, Massachusetts.

Frank CHONG grew up in central California, graduated from the U.S. Naval Academy, and served as a nuclear engineer in the U.S. Navy before joining the U-M MBA/MA in Asian Studies program (1999). Frank then worked as a product manager for Lucent Technologies and a product line manager for Centerpoint Broadband Technologies before joining Northrup Grumman Space Technology as a lead engineer. In 2007, he became Director, Quality, Safety and Mission Assurance for Advanced Concepts Space and Directed Energy at Northrup Grumman Aerospace Systems, based in the Los Angeles area where he lives with his wife and two daughters.

Peter CHRISTIAN obtained a BA in history from Cornell and the MBA/MA in Asian Studies from U-M (1989). Peter worked at NSK Corp. in Ann Arbor as a customer service representative, manufacturing operations analyst, and quality engineer, before moving to New Jersey in 2005 to work as a quality engineer at Alcoa Investing Castings and Forge Products, A. Raymond Timmerman Manufacturing, and OXO. In 2011, he became Regulatory Compliance Manager at Igloo Products in the Houston, Texas, area.

Alexandra CONROY Baig obtained a BA in English from the University of Chicago and the MBA/MA in Asian Studies from U-M (1999). Alex worked in Hong Kong and Shanghai in equity research for Barings before returning to the United States to study at the Catholic Theological Union at Chicago. She is a Certified Financial Planner and works as a financial advisor in the Chicago area, with a special interest in helping individuals and families with disabilities.

Jason CONWAY graduated with a BA in Economics from Cornell University. After four years working in investment banking, Jason spent two years teaching finance at Shanghai University. He completed his U-M MBA/MA in Asian Studies in 2002 and has since worked in financial technology product management and sales, first for ConvergEx, where he helped develop a platform for electronic trading of equities on global exchanges, primarily in Asia. He joined TradingScreen in 2010 to develop the company's electronic trading capabilities for listed securities. He currently manages an investment accounting application targeted to large global insurers for SS&C Technologies. Jason lives in Simsbury, Connecticut, with his wife Tiffany (U-M MBA, 2001) and their three daughters.

Wm Patrick CRANLEY studied the economics and politics of the People's Republic of China at Brown University, the Hopkins-Nanjing Center, and U-M, where he was one of the earliest MBA/MA in Asian Studies graduates (1988). In 1995, he moved to China as Chief Representative of CIGNA Corporation, where he worked from 1988 to 2001, when he founded and is Managing Director of AsiaMedia, a China-focused marketing strategy and public relations agency. He served on the board of the American Chamber of Commerce in Shanghai for five years, including a year as Chairman in 2000. Patrick is one of the founders of Historic Shanghai, a group dedicated to research and raising awareness of the city's social, economic, and architectural heritage. He has appeared on China Central Television, the BBC, CNN, NPR, the Canadian Broadcasting Corporation, CBS News Sunday Morning, and many documentary films. Patrick is a member of the National Council on U.S.-China Relations and a board member of the International Coalition of Art Deco Societies.

Michael (Mike) DUNNE (also CSEAS), a native of the Detroit area, obtained his BA and MBA/MA in Asian Studies from U-M, where he studied Chinese and Thai. In 1993, in Bangkok, he founded Automotive Resources Asia (ARA) to provide consulting services to multinational automotive companies, later opening an office in Shanghai. In 2006, he sold ARA to J.D. Power and Associates, becoming its VP for Asia-Pacific and MD for China until 2010. In 2011, Mike published the well-reviewed book *American Wheels, Chinese Roads*, then served as President of General Motors Indonesia from 2013 until GM withdrew from that market in 2015. A frequent columnist and sought-after speaker at corporate events, Mike is now working on a book on Chinese cars coming to the U.S. market. He divides his time between Asia, where his Hong Kong–based marketing consultancy Dunne Automotive works with automakers and suppliers, and San Diego, California, where his wife, Merlien, and their three children reside.

Amy Rubin FRIEL (also CSEAS) grew up in Michigan and obtained degrees from Northwestern University (BS) and U-M

(MBA/MA in Asian Studies), where she studied Chinese and Indonesian languages. She began her marketing career at Procter & Gamble, then ran a business at Dole Foods before moving to Asia. Amy transitioned to tech while in Singapore and for more than five years held multiple leadership roles in digital marketing and advertising for Intel Asia-Pacific. After several more years with global tech giants, Amy shifted focus to digital health, launching Nokia's new health business and a variety of start-ups. She's currently VP of Marketing for Tidepool.org, a tech non-profit developing tools for people with Type 1 diabetes. Amy also advises start-ups in the multi-trillion dollar global "longevity economy." A lifelong competitive athlete, Amy trains for triathlons and marathons. She lives in San Jose, California, with her husband, Pat, and pack of retired racing Greyhounds.

Thomas HORN graduated with a BBA in Finance from Texas A&M University, during which he spent a year learning language at the National Taiwan Normal University. He obtained the MBA/MA in Asian Studies from U-M (1997), after which he joined J.P. Morgan in investment banking (New York and Hong Kong, 1998–2002), becoming VP, then Executive Director and Global Head for Strategy and Business Development (New York, 2002–2008). In 2008, Tom moved to Singapore as Executive Director, Global Commodities Principal Investments, then moved to Beijing as Executive Director, Commodity Finance and Structuring. In 2013, Tom joined Barclays Investment Bank as Head of Commodity Finance for Asia-Pacific, moving on to ANZ

Bank as Head of Structured Trade Finance for North Asia. Since 2015, he has been Executive Director, Natural Resources Group, for the Commonwealth Bank of Australia, based in Hong Kong.

Simon KAHN obtained a BS in Asian Studies from Swarthmore College, then worked in Washington, DC, before enrolling in the U-M MBA/MA in Asian Studies program (1998), after which he joined American Express in New York, and in 2008 was posted to Singapore as its Country Manager. Since 2011, Simon has been Google's Chief Marketing Officer for Asia Pacific, based in Singapore where he lives with his wife and their three children.

Scott LABADIE graduated from Michigan State University with a BS in Computer Science and East Asian Studies, and obtained from U-M an MA in Asian Studies (2003), after which he interned at the U.S. Foreign and Commercial Service in Beijing and attended the Guanghua School of Management at Peking University. Scott obtained the U-M MBA (2010) during his 10-year stint as a project lead for application systems and programming at General Dynamics Land Systems in the Detroit area. In 2011, he moved to Seattle, Washington, as Technical Program Manager, then Software Development Manager, for

Amazon. Since 2016, he has been Software Development Manager for Amazon Web Services.

Michael (Mike) F. LITTLE Jr. has been speaking Mandarin Chinese for 32 years and is still not sure what to say. Originally from New Orleans, he has been living in Asia off and on since 1994. After graduating from Oberlin College in Chinese literature and U-M in Asian Studies and the MBA, he worked for United Technologies (Carrier) and Ford Motor, among others, in regional and global roles. Working mainly in the world of purchasing, Mike tries to divine what is going on in the minds of Asian suppliers while growing and developing teams across cultures. Recently relocated to Bangkok after being based in Shanghai for six years, he currently leads a team of 65 Indian, Australian, Thai, and Chinese colleagues across five Asian countries and enjoys spending time with his four children.

Paul LOWREY received his BA in Philosophy from Haverford College and the MBA/MA in Asian Studies from U-M (1988), after which he moved to the San Francisco Bay Area, where he remains. Paul worked for seven years as Director of Marketing for Plextor Americas, a subsidiary of Shinano Kenshi of Japan, managing its major OEM accounts with U.S. tech companies. He continued in sales and marketing functions for Embark Corp. and SinoProjects before becoming Director of Marketing for NewRetirement.com in 2005 until 2016. Paul has served concurrently as digital marketing consultant for Torad Consulting since 2002.

Tom ROSENTHAL obtained his BA and MBA/MA in Asian Studies from U-M (1995) and has since been a serial entrepreneur. Tom first co-founded MeetChina.com, an e-commerce platform (and Alibaba precursor) that lasted seven years (they were too early!), before moving on to co-found China New Media, based in Shenzhen. In 2012, Tom returned to the United States, settling with his two sons in La Jolla, California, where he co-founded pixtas.com.

Joel SAMUELS obtained the U-M MBA in 1989, completing the MA in Asian Studies in 1999. A California native and former ski instructor, he obtained his JD at the UC Davis School of Law in 2004, served as Deputy District Attorney for Inyo county, and since 2014 has been Deputy Attorney-General for California, based in Sacramento. Joel lives in Davis, California, with his wife and two daughters and practices his "bad Chinese" on waiters in Chinese restaurants.

Wesley SEALAND has a BA in History from Stanford and the MBA/MA in Asian Studies from U-M (1993). From 2000 to 2012, he worked at Novellus Systems in Oregon, as Senior Account Executive, Director of Sales, and Senior Director of Business Development, before joining Lam Research, a global supplier of semiconductor manufacturing equipment and services to the world's leading chipmakers. Wes serves as Lam's Senior Director of Product Group Marketing and Business Development, based in Oregon.

Benjamin SIMAR grew up in Texas and graduated from the University of Texas-Austin with dual degrees in business administration and liberal arts, where he double majored in Spanish and Portuguese and minored in Chinese, following up with a year's language study in Taiwan. Ben then worked as a security and audit manager for SGS in Shenzhen and in brand protection operations for Hill and Associates in Shanghai before enrolling in the U-M MBA/MA in Asian Studies program (2004). He wrote his master's thesis on Macau's reversion to China, drawing on Portuguese as well as Chinese and English sources. He returned to work in security and corporate investigation at Bechtel (Huizhou), Wynn (Macau), and Control Risks (Shanghai), where he became Director, Consulting for Greater China and North Asia. In 2012, Ben became Director, Security, Asia Pacific for Johnson Controls, based in Shanghai, and in 2015, he moved with his wife to Hong Kong as Senior Director, Brand Protection and Security, for Flextronics. Ben enjoys participating in U-M alumni activities throughout the Asia Pacific.

Tom STANLEY grew up mostly in Michigan and obtained his BA in Chinese Language and Literature and his MBA (1993) from U-M. After several years working in a U.S.-China Automotive JV in Eastern China, he has worked for KPMG since 1996, in Hong Kong and mostly in Shanghai, where he worked in management consulting and in the Deal Advisory practice focusing on China market entry projects, including inbound M&A. Tom is now Partner, Chief Knowledge Officer, and Chief Operating Office, Markets to KPMG China.

Joan STEPHENSON obtained her BA in East Asian Studies and English Literature from Vanderbilt University, then worked in Taipei for several years before enrolling in the U-M MBA/MA in Asian Studies program (1997). She has been a management consultant for IBM and is now a partner, based in New York City.

Charles Dever TODD obtained his BS and MBA/MA in Asian Studies (1989) from U-M.

Nancy YU Kochansky was born in New Orleans and grew up

in Huntsville, Alabama. She obtained a BA in Comparative Area Studies (Asia) and French Literature from Duke, during which she studied abroad in Nanjing and Beijing. Upon graduation, Nancy taught English and studied Chinese in Taipei before earning the U-M MBA/MA in Asian Studies (1994), after which she worked for the China Strategy Group at Coopers & Lybrand Consulting. She then spent nine years at Morgan Stanley in New York City as a pharmaceutical analyst and as Associate Director of Research in charge of North American research associates. She also served as an adjunct instructor in business at Concordia College in New York, as a global pharmaceutical analyst at Magnestar Capital, and as COO at ViaBay Capital, a start-up healthcare investment fund. She currently works at Memorial Sloan-Kettering Cancer Center's Center for Health Policy and Outcomes, focusing on drug pricing issues. Nancy and her husband, Jody, live in Bronxville, New York, with their four children aged 8–16 years. She maintains her strong interest in China and Mandarin proficiency.

Eric ZWISLER graduated from Carroll University (BS Economics, 1980) and U-M (MBA, 1982), where he also completed coursework for the MA in Asian Studies (China) (1987). He has been involved in healthcare businesses in Asia and particularly China for the last 29 years as President of Cardinal Health China, CEO of Zuellig Pharma Asia Pacific, and currently Chairman of Cardinal Health China. Eric has been recognized by the highest levels of the Chinese government for his contributions to business and society, including the Friendship

Medal (2008), the highest national level award bestowed on foreigners in China. He is also an Honorary Citizen of Shanghai (2004), silver and gold Magnolia Medal honoree, and one of the first foreigners given permanent residence in China, where he and his wife, Tori, have lived for most of their 30 years in Asia.

MBA/MA IN ASIAN STUDIES (CENTER FOR JAPANESE STUDIES)

Aundrea ALMOND has a BA in East Asian Studies from Wesleyan University, after which she was as a consular official at the Consulate-General of Japan in Detroit before enrolling in the U-M MBA/MA in Asian Studies program (2001). Aundrea then worked as a training and organizational development specialist for Medtronic in Minneapolis, California, Tokyo, and the Netherlands. She continued to work in organizational development for Synthes Inc. and eBay Enterprise before becoming Director of Organizational Development for Radial Inc. in King of Prussia, Pennsylvania, since 2016.

Brendan BUESCHER graduated in mathematics from Amherst College, then served in the U.S. Air Force before obtaining the MBA/MA in Asian Studies from U-M, after which he joined McKinsey and Co. Since 2010, he has been senior partner and managing partner of McKinsey's Cleveland/Akron office, with a special focus on helping healthcare organizations develop and deliver strategies for change, growth, and innovation.

Christopher DEROSE obtained his MBA/MA in Asian Studies from U-M in 1996 and works in management consulting in the Detroit area.

LeAnn ERIKSSON grew up in Iowa and obtained her BGS in Asian Studies and Linguistics from the University of Iowa (1984), after which she managed international relations for the Japan Health Center Corp. in the Kansai before enrolling in the U-M MBA/MA in Asian Studies program (1991). LeAnn then worked as a financial analyst for Procter & Gamble in Cincinnati and was a consultant for Bain & Co. in Tokyo before returning to Ann Arbor, where she freelance consulted on several Japan-related projects. After becoming a mother, she organized and participated in many musical activities, including as board member of a chamber music festival and flute player in an English country and contra dance band. LeAnn later co-created Wavegarden and Deep Wild Stillness, original music based on crystal singing bowls, flutes, and voice that brings listeners into relaxation and altered states. She now also co-facilitates Voice Awakening playshops, vibrational baths, and private sessions worldwide with her partner and continues to write music (using the artistic name of Taralian) between her bases in Cologne, Germany, and Bali, Indonesia. She and Jeff Guyton (also MBA/MA, 1991) share two world-traveling, multilingual daughters.

Michelle Lynn GROSS obtained her BA and MBA/MA in Asian Studies (1990) at U-M.

Jeffrey GUYTON, a native of Akron, Ohio, graduated with a BA in Chemistry and Asian Studies from the University of Wittenberg in Ohio (1988) and was admitted to medical school (like his doctor father, uncle, and brother) but turned it down to enroll in U-M's MA in Asian Studies program. He was twice rejected for the MBA due to lack of work experience but succeeded in his third try due to persistence and a recommendation from Professor Linda Lim. In 1991, Jeff became the first foreign national hired as a local in Ford Motor Japan, where he was a financial analyst based in Hiroshima and Tokyo. After returning to Dearborn in 1994 as a finance manager for Ford, in 2000, Jeff became the youngest manager ever (at age 35) to become an executive officer of Mazda Motor, which in 2003 posted him to Germany as Vice-President and CFO, then in 2009 as President and CEO, of Mazda Motor Europe. Together with LeAnn Eriksson (also MBA/MA, 1991), he has two world-traveling, multilingual daughters.

Neil HARRISON obtained a BA in International Relations and Asian and Middle Eastern Studies from the University of Pennsylvania and the MBA/MA in Asian Studies from U-M (2005), both with a continued focus on Japan. Neil started his career as a management consultant, working in the technology, media, and telecommunications practice of Diamond Management & Technology Consultants (now part of PwC Advisory Services).While at Diamond, he assisted clients such as AT&T, Time Warner, AOL, Sprint, Motorola, Mitsubishi Electric, the City of New York, Morgan Stanley, Goldman Sachs, and the private equity firm of Clayton, Dubilier & Rice with strategy and operations issues related to innovation, emerging technologies, digital disruption, and the growth of the internet and mobile devices. He joined Sony Corporation of America in 2008, where he currently serves as Senior Director, Corporate Programs & Initiatives. In this role, Neil supports members of Sony Corporation of America's senior management team and has a variety of responsibilities, including involvement in corporate planning, operations, and risk management. Neil also serves on the board of Older Adults Technology Services (OATS), a non-profit that harnesses the power of technology to change the way we age. He lives on Long Island with his wife, Wendy, and two sons.

Daniel HEILBRUNN obtained a BSE from Duke, then worked as a project engineer for Mitsubishi Semiconductor America for four years before enrolling in U-M's MBA/MA in Asian Studies program (1998), after which he worked in marketing at Guidant for eight years. Dan then became VP for Marketing and Business Development at Nexeon MedSystems and VP for Portfolio Management at CeloNova Biosciences Inc. before becoming Senior Consultant and President of SPRIG Consulting in Vancouver, Canada. Since 2014, he has also been VP for Marketing and Business Development, and a board member, of BrightWater Medical.

Simone HERON graduated from the University of Texas-Austin McCombs School of Business, where she was President of the Japanese Culture Club and studied abroad in Tokyo. She was a sales analyst at General Mills in Minnesota before enrolling in the U-M MBA/MA in Asian Studies program (2008), during which she did marketing internships at Johnson & Johnson and Kraft Foods. Simone then worked as a brand manager for Reckitt Benckiser, and for Kao USA, before moving to New York where she is now Director of Marketing, Hair Care for LF Beauty/ Lornamead, a Li & Fung company.

Leroy HOWARD obtained his BA and MBA/MA in Asian Studies (1991) from U-M. He now takes care of the home front while his wife Dana Buntrock (U-M Master of Architecture) teaches at the University of California, Berkeley and researches Japanese architecture. Leroy's own photographic work most recently consists of The Women's Last Supper Project (www.leroyhoward.com) and includes 25 images of buildings under construction on the UC Berkeley campus, in the Bancroft Library.

Arif IQBALL grew up in Pakistan and received degrees in engineering from Clemson (BS Mechanical) and Northwestern (MS Manufacturing) universities, after which he worked for Ford Motor Company in Dearborn, Michigan, as a test engineer. Arif earned the MBA/MA in Asian Studies at U-M (1995), then worked on an expatriate assignment with Ford/Mazda in Hiroshima, Japan, for a year. In 1999, he joined Delphi as the

Asia-Pacific (AP) Senior Finance Manager and returned to Japan, becoming country CFO and eventually adding AP strategic planning responsibilities. Arif then turned to consumer industries, joining in succession Avon Japan, Nippon Becton Dickinson, and McCann Worldgroup Holdings, mostly in finance and strategy roles, before becoming Global CFO and Corporate SVP for Benesse Holdings, a Tier 1 Japanese public company in the education business. In 2016, Arif started teaching Leadership and Finance at Kansai Gaidai University and is getting certified as an Executive Coach. He and his wife are based in Kyoto, Japan.

Bruce IRISH holds BS and MS degrees in Computer Science and the MBA/MA in Asian Studies (1993) from U-M. He worked as Worldwide Market Development Manager for Sun Microsystems and as Group Marketing Manager for Microsoft, after which he was co-founder and VP of Business Development for Cross Pharmaceuticals, VP for Marketing and Product Strategy for Gamma Enterprise Technologies (now Informatica), and founder and President of Thira Corporation (2002–2011), a profitable global trade and investment firm focused on China and serving customers in Japan, Europe, and the United States. Since 2010, Bruce has been an angel investor with Tech Coast Angels, which funds mostly emerging technologies and life sciences companies. He lives in Newbury Park, California, with his wife, Jian, and their son.

Scot KOJOLA graduated from the University of Cincinnati with a BE in Chemical Engineering, after which he worked as a research engineer for Kao Corporation for five years before enrolling in U-M's MBA/MA in Asian Studies program (2003). Scot then went to work for American Express in Greensboro/Winter-Salem, North Carolina, where he has served in the Global Business Travel division as Business Transformation Manager, Director of Information Systems, Director of Revenue Management, Director of Billing, and since 2016 as Director of the Transformation Partner Network.

A Rama KRISHNA obtained a BA (Honors) in Economics from St. Stephen's College and an MBA/MA in Asian Studies (Japan Specialization) from U-M (1987). He was Chief Investment Strategist and Director-Equity Research for Credit Suisse First Boston; Director of International Equity Research and Chief Investment Officer-Emerging Markets, Portfolio Manager-Global/International Equities for AllianceBernstein; then Chief Investment Officer and Head (institutional and international) for Citigroup Asset Management, where he also represented the business on the Citigroup Management Committee before becoming President-International and Managing Principal for Pzena Investment Management. In 2010, Rama founded and is Chief Investment Officer of ARGA Investment Management, which invests in global equities including in emerging markets, based in Stamford, Connecticut.

James (Jim) LANNEN has a BA in Mathematics, an MA in Actuarial Science (1968), and an MA in Asian Studies (1991) from U-M. During his career, Jim worked for TIAA-CREF, Aeroquip Corp., a manufacturing firm, and two international management consulting firms that are now part of Willis Towers Watson. Jim has been retired for several years, and he and his wife, Laurel, recently moved back to Chicago.

    Keith LUBLIN obtained his BS in Psychology and Economics from Duke and the MBA/MA in Asian Studies from U-M (1995), then was Assistant VP at Citibank Tokyo before becoming VP at J.P. Morgan Chase in Detroit. Keith now works at Level One Bank in the greater Detroit area.

Paul **MARTIN** obtained a BA from the University of Massachusetts-Amherst and the MBA/MA in Asian Studies from U-M (1990). He worked in various roles at Continental Bank, Visa International, Cyberbills, Metavante, Digital Insight, and Intuit Financial Services before joining Wells Fargo in 2010 as VP, Solution Sales, Treasury Management, becoming Senior VP in 2015. Paul lives in San Francisco with his wife, Eileen; their two children are in college.

Andrew **MASTERMAN** grew up in Oregon, obtaining a BA from Colorado College (1989) and the MBA/MA in Asian Studies and MS in Industrial Engineering from U-M (1993). Andrew then joined Intel Corp. in Portland before moving to Tokyo as President of Walbro Japan, Singapore and Walbro Asia, from 1995–1999, during which he had full P&L responsibility for a $100m automotive and small engine fuel systems business in Japan, Korea, and China. When Walbro was sold to TI Automotive, Andrew became an officer in the company and relocated to Tucson, Arizona. In 2005, he was recruited to become President and COO of Spartan Light Metal Products, then President of Platinum Group Metals for Metallico, and from 2009–2012, President and CEO North America ($500m revenue) for the UK's ESAB Group. Andrew then joined Precision Castparts (PCP) as President of its Fastener Division ($1.4b), Airframe Products Segment ($3b), and Wyman Gordon and Structural Castings Segments ($3.6b), also serving as Executive VP. In 2016, he became CEO of Brightview Landscapes LLC, the world's largest landscaping company with over \$2.2b in revenue and 22,000 employees, based in Philadelphia. Andrew and his wife, Cheryl, live in Villanova, Pennsylvania, and have three children in high school and college.

Ashley McCORKLE obtained a BA in International Affairs and Economics from George Washington University and the MBA/ MA in Asian Studies from U-M (1993). He joined Intel Corp. in Santa Clara, California, in 1997, holding successive roles as Brand Research Analyst, New Product Research Analyst, UX Research Manager, Compute Continuum Experience Strategist, and User Insights Innovation Manager (since 2011).

David MOST graduated in industrial engineering from Northwestern and from U-M's MBA/MA in Asian Studies program (1992). Since 2003, he has been VP for marketing for the Manischewitz Co., the largest U.S. manufacturer of processed kosher food products, based in New Jersey, where Dave volunteers as an organizer for the Community Food Bank of New Jersey and for the Home for Good Dog Rescue.

Nancy Ann NETTLETON obtained her BA and MBA/MA in

Asian Studies (1988) from U-M and in 2000 went to work for Dell Computer in Texas.

Adam ORLAN obtained a BS in Economics from the State University of New York at Albany, then worked as an economist in New York before enrolling in U-M's MBA/MA in Asian Studies program (1989). Adam has worked in HR and HR client consulting ever since, for ARCO Chemical, Citibank, and from 1999–2014 at Capital One, mostly in Richmond, Virginia, where he led the company's organizational change management function. Since 2015, Adam has been VP of Human Resources at Connexion Loyalty, also in Richmond.

Joseph (Joe) OSHA obtained a BA in Finance from the University of Richmond and the MBA/MA in Asian Studies from U-M (1992), after which he joined Baring Securities in Tokyo as an equity research analyst, moving to New York in 1997, and San Francisco in 2000, to cover semiconductors for Merrill Lynch. In 2007, he became Head of Asia Equity Research for Bank of America Merrill Lynch based in Hong Kong, returning to the Bay

Area in 2011 to head alternative energy research for BAML. Joe next served as CFO and Advisor to two alternative energy start-ups, Gravity Renewables and Greenfire Energy, before becoming Managing Director of Equity Research for JMP Securities covering industrial and energy technology companies. Joe lives in the San Francisco Bay Area with his wife, Stephanie (U-M JD, 1992), and their two children. He is a volunteer board member for the Lincoln Child Center in Oakland, which has been serving at-risk youth and their families for 130 years.

Jeffrey PROTZEL obtained his BA in Computer Science from New York University (1982) after also studying mathematics and computer science at Clark University. He studied Japanese language and taught English in Japan before enrolling in U-M's MBA/MA in Asian Studies program (1989), specializing in real estate finance. He was a consultant and board member of Design Associates, a commercial real estate firm in Louisiana, for seven years, then continued to work as an independent contractor and at Wayne Pugh and Associates before establishing his own independent commercial appraisal firm, Protzel and Associates, in 2016. Jeff lives with his wife, Lumie, and two daughters in Slidell, Louisiana, near New Orleans.

David QUIGLEY obtained his MBA/MA in Asian Studies from U-M in 1983 and started his international career overseas in Japan, Belgium, Luxembourg, and the Philippines with Goodyear International Tire Co., and then represented the U.S. government and the U.S. meat industry as the Director of Asia for the U.S. Meat Export Federation. He later started an entrepreneurial medical device business with Japan Biomedical Search in South Bend, Indiana, and now he has over 25 years in the medical device field with Focus Surgery and Accordion Medical. He has operated in these companies as an investor and board member in his capacity as the President of THS International since 1996. Dave specializes in turning around bankrupt medical device companies and launching new medical products globally.

James (Jim) ROCHE has a BA in Political Science from Williams College and an MBA/MA in Asian Studies from U-M (1989). He worked as regional sales manager for Sony Electronics, then as sales and customer service representative for Japan Airlines before joining United Airlines in 2003 as sales manager in Chicago, where he remains.

Paul SCHOMBURG obtained a BA in Asian Studies from Northwestern, after which he served in the U.S. Navy before enrolling in U-M's MBA/MA in Asian Studies program (1988). He worked as Assistant Planning Manager for Panasonic Communications & Systems in New Jersey before moving to Washington, DC, in 1994 as Director of Government and Public Affairs for Panasonic Corporation of North America. Paul is active in many community and industry activities, including coordination of Panasonic relationships with Congress and regulatory agencies, and liaisons with high-tech industry associations and consumer groups. In 2012, he participated in international relief efforts to aid reconstruction of Ishinomaki after the 2011 earthquake and tsunami.

Donald SEMONES obtained a BS in Chemical Engineering from the University of Cincinnati, after which he served as a submarine officer in the U.S. Navy for eight years before enrolling in U-M's MBA/MA in Asian Studies program (1997). Since then Don has worked for Dexter Fastener Technologies in Dexter, Michigan, as Special Projects Engineer, Sales Manager, Steel Buyer, Plant Engineer, and since 2011 as Environmental, Health, and Safety Manager. Don lives in Ann Arbor with his wife, Seiko, their twin daughters, and two Samoyed dogs.

Cynthia TRAGGE-LAKRA has a BA in Political Science and an MBA/MA in Asian Studies from U-M (1993), after which she pursued entrepreneurial ventures in China and Japan and managed her family's U.S. telecommunications business. Cynthia then joined GE's Human Leadership Program and Corporate Audit Staff, serving in a variety of functions, industries, and global locations over 20 years, including as SVP, HR for GE Money Americas leading a workforce of 25,000 across 12 countries and SVP, HR for GE Capital Global Equipment Services & Consumer Finance managing a workforce of 13,000 across 26 countries. Cynthia led the HR transition efforts related to Synchrony Financial's IPO and separation from GE and now leads Synchrony's Talent, Learning and Culture Practice as its SVP and Chief Talent Officer. A frequent speaker on organizational change, culture, and executive development, she lives in Connecticut with her husband, Rajeev Lakra (U-M MBA, 1991), and children and serves on advisory boards with Linkage Women in Leadership and Norwalk Community College.

David WHETSTONE obtained a BS in Accounting and Economics at the University of Illinois, and the MBA/MA in Asian Studies from U-M (1990/1991). He worked in consulting for Bain and Price Waterhouse, then as Group Director, Marketing for Air Touch before founding and serving as CMO for Virgin Mobile, a virtual mobile network operator, in 2000. Dave was VP, Global Marketing for WebEx Communications and CMO for MobiTV. In 2006, he became CEO of Brand Mobility, a mobile/social product design and development firm that builds iPhone and Android applications for leading brands. Dave lives in San Francisco with his wife, Irene (U-M BA, 1985), and their two daughters.

Robert (Bob) WILSON grew up in Mississippi and Okinawa, Japan. After graduating with a BS in Chemical Engineering from Michigan Technological University, he worked in technical sales for Shell Chemical and in marketing for Mitsubishi Rayon before enrolling in U-M's MBA/MA in Asian Studies program (1998). After working in management consulting with Arthur D. Little and for two tech start-ups, in 2002, he joined W.R. Grace in

Boston and from 2007 to 2010 ran the North Asia P&L for Grace's construction business based out of Tokyo. He returned to Boston as Vice-President of Marketing for Grace's performance chemicals division. Bob is now Vice-President of Marketing at Swagelok, a $1.8b privately held company that develops and provides high-quality fluid system solutions for global customers in the oil and gas, power, petrochemical, alternative fuels, semiconductor, and other industries. Swagelok is headquartered in Solon, Ohio, where Bob enjoys living with his wife, Julie, and their two daughters and is active in community activities including serving as past President of the Rotary Club and on the board of trustees of the Cleveland Institute of Music.

Ali ZAMIRI grew up in the Detroit area, obtaining a BA in Economics and an MBA/MA in Asian Studies (1991) from U-M. He worked in Japan as a brand manager for Sunstar Inc. in oral hygiene products, where he had to undergo the rigorous training and lifestyle (living in a company dorm!) of a *shinyuushaiin* at a Japanese corporation from 1991–1994. He then joined Adidas Japan as a product manager for footwear from 1994–1997, where he had the chance to take a tennis lesson with Steffi Graf. Since 1998, Ali's job in international business development for Qualcomm has seen him take leading roles in China, Middle East, and Africa. Recently, responding to his son's request, he has given up the extensive travel required of those positions to focus on developing the Internet of Things in North America, but he still finds time to get back to China to meet with device vendors in this space. Ali continues to enjoy living in San Diego, playing tennis, and surfing the waves at Torrey Pines year-round. He would greatly enjoy hosting a mini-reunion in SoCal one of these days!

Paul ZIOTS holds a BSE in Industrial and Operations Engineering and an MBA/MA in Asian Studies from U-M (1994), after which he was Finance and Commodity Manager for General Motors before moving to California as Director of Investor Relations for Sun Microsystems from 1995–2010. Paul then served as Director of Investor Relations for Oracle before assuming in 2012 his current position as VP for Investor Relations for VMWare, the global leader in virtualization and cloud infrastructure, based in Palo Alto, California.

MBA/MA IN ASIAN STUDIES (CENTER FOR SOUTHEAST ASIAN STUDIES)

Jon BLUMENAUER grew up in Portland, Oregon, played basketball and baseball, and upon graduation from Pomona

College, joined hometown company Nike, which soon posted him to Asia to manage its contract factories in Singapore, Malaysia, and Sri Lanka. After nine years with Nike in four different countries, Jon came to U-M for the MBA/MA, during which he studied Thai and Indonesian languages. After graduating in 2002, he worked briefly in Indonesia, then in Thailand and Belgium as Director of Asia and then of International Operations for GAS International, a security company. Jon then became a sustainability strategies consultant based in Portland, where he eventually became CEO of The Joinery, which designs and manufactures hardwood furniture using sustainable methods. Jon lives with his wife, a native of Burkina Faso, and their two children, traveling to Thailand frequently to visit friends.

Paul CHURCHILL grew up in Manila, Jakarta, Canberra, and Washington, DC, then graduated from Dartmouth College in history and Asian studies and from U-M with the MBA/MA in Asian Studies, studying Indonesian language. Paul worked in marketing for Procter & Gamble Europe from 1994 to 2003, first in Vienna (thanks to his Austrian wife Elisabeth), followed by Geneva and Frankfurt, before moving to the Campbell's Soup Company in Cambridge, UK. Having always been active with various sports, Paul then moved to Nuremberg to work for PUMA Europe, after which he moved to Munich with Red Bull (an "incredibly fun" job). Paul has recently taken a new role as global head of marketing for Suunto, a Finnish GPS sports watch and dive computer company that is part of the larger

Amer Sports group. Over the years he has made business trips to Southeast Asia, China, and Japan and enjoys the regular Asia involvement in his new role. His family have enjoyed regular vacations in the Philippines, and remain in Munich with their German-English bilingual teenage sons.

Steven (Steve) Don DEAN grew up in Michigan and obtained degrees from Wheaton College (BA English) and U-M (MBA/ MA in Asian Studies), where he studied Indonesian language and finance. He went to Singapore in 1989 to work in marketing for Gerber Foods before returning to various roles in finance, including stockbroking and banking for private clients. In 2006, he joined Thomson Reuters in Singapore, becoming Head of Account Management focusing on digital banking. Steve now resides with his wife, June, in Jakarta where he heads Thomson Reuters' operations in Indonesia. Their son, Brendan, graduated from Harvard in 2019.

Michael (Mike) DUNNE (also CCS) see biography in CCS section above.

Amy Rubin FRIEL (also CCS) see biography in CCS section above.

Patrick FRIEL grew up in Ohio, graduating from The Ohio State University (1987) with a BA in Middle Eastern Studies, which included a year at The American University in Cairo. Pat then went as a Fulbright scholar to the University of Jordan to further his studies of Arabic language before joining the U-M MBA/MA in Asian Studies program, during which he managed to study Thai, Indonesian, and Vietnamese! He worked successively for Monroe Auto Equipment, Dole Foods, and Tenneco Automotive Asia in a variety of financial, marketing, and operational roles before becoming Manager of Far East Internal Audit for Intel Technology Asia, based in Singapore. Since 2001, Pat has been investing and trading in stocks, futures, and options to produce market beating returns for 16 years! He lives in San Jose, California, with his wife, Amy, and their retired racing Greyhounds.

Martha Masterman GORDON grew up in La Grande, Oregon, and obtained a BA in International Affairs from Lewis and Clark College (1992), after which she taught English as a second language in Salatiga, Indonesia, before enrolling in U-M's MBA/

MA in Asian Studies program (1999), when she studied Indonesian language. Martha then worked in marketing for the Campbell Soup Company before returning to Ann Arbor as Consulting Manager, then Vice-President, for GfK Strategic Innovation. Since 2014, she has worked as a freelance marketing consultant on brand growth strategies for a variety of local and regional companies. Martha lives in Ann Arbor with her husband, Scott, and their two children and volunteers as a board member for Ten Thousand Villages, a national fair trade retailer.

Patrick J. GRIFFIN grew up in Evansville, Indiana, and obtained his BA in History and Economics from Trinity University (1992) and the MBA/MA in Asian Studies from U-M (1998), where he studied Indonesian language. Patrick worked in strategic planning for Koch Industries in Wichita, Kansas, then moved to Austin, Texas, joining the start-up bottomdollar.com, which was successfully sold to Network Commerce in Seattle. He then joined Escalade Inc., an Evansville-based sporting goods company. Patrick moved to Germany for five years with Escalade Inc. and eventually led their subsidiary there. He returned to Evansville as Escalade's Vice-President of Corporate Development and Investor Relations, leading multiple acquisitions and divestitures. Patrick serves on the board of directors for Escalade and Stiga Sports, a Swedish sporting goods company which is increasing its presence in Japan and China. He enjoys being involved in various community activities in Evansville, where his wife, Jill (U-M MBA/MS Industrial Engineering, 1998), is Executive Director of the Institute for

Global Enterprise in Indiana at the University of Evansville, and their two children work hard to maintain their German language.

Mark GUTHRIE grew up in Terre Haute, Indiana, graduating with degrees in civil and environmental engineering from Duke (BSE, 1978) and Purdue (MSCE, 1983), after which he worked as a project engineer, project manager, and manager of industrial waste services for Engineering-Science Inc. in Atlanta, Georgia, and (from 1987) in Bangkok, Thailand. In 1995, Mark moved to Parsons Engineering Science's International Division in Manila, Philippines, as their Asia Regional Manager for Industrial Services before enrolling in the U-M MBA/MA in Asian Studies program (2002). He returned to live in Bangkok, working on various international assignments as an independent consultant on environmental engineering infrastructure and corporate financial advisory services. Mark has worked throughout the Middle East and Asia, including Japan, Korea, Taiwan, China, India, Philippines, Indonesia, Malaysia, Thailand, Vietnam, Singapore, and Sri Lanka.

Michael HELMUS obtained his MBA/MA in Asian Studies from U-M (1994). During the program he studied Indonesian and worked two internships in Jakarta, with Pharmacia/Upjohn and Wrigley's. Upon graduation, Michael returned to the accounting profession, working sequentially for PricewaterhouseCoopers, Provident Bank, U.S. Bank, and First Financial Holdings in audit and enterprise risk management.

Nathan JOHNSON grew up in North Carolina and graduated from Brown University (AB Economics). He then spent two years teaching English at Gadjah Mada University in Yogyakarta, Indonesia, with the Princeton-in-Asia program. Returning to the United States, he became one of the initial students in U-M's MBA/MA joint program. In 1987, Nathan started in product management at AT&T Network Systems (later Lucent Technologies), and in 1994 was assigned to Indonesia. When Lucent withdrew from Indonesia in 2001, several senior managers at Lucent Indonesia established Lintas Teknologi as a systems integrator to resell Lucent (and later other) products. Lintas has become one of Indonesia's largest systems integrators focused on the telecommunications market. Nathan continues to work at Lintas and lives in Jakarta with his wife, Retno (Eri) Hapsari.

Brendan KAVANEY grew up in St. Paul, Minnesota, and attended college at St. Olaf, where he majored in economics, played football, and studied abroad in Europe, the Middle East, India/Nepal, China, South Korea, and Southeast Asia. Upon graduating in 1997, he moved to Thailand where he studied in Chiang Mai, taught English in Khon Kaen, and worked for *The Economist* in Bangkok. After seven years in Thailand, he moved to U-M for the MBA/MA in Asian Studies, graduating in 2007 and taking a job with HCL, a large Indian IT services company. He then spent two years at Infosys and is currently a Marketing Director with Mindtree, a midsized Indian firm, where he works closely with the CMO and runs all aspects of marketing and sales operations. Brendan lives with his wife, Pepper, an advertising industry veteran, and their daughter in San Francisco, traveling to India and Thailand every year.

Audrey KING grew up in New York and studied Thai for her U-M MBA/MA in Asian Studies. After graduating in 1986, she joined Data-General in human resources management and is now Corporate Compensation Manager at a successor company, Teradyne, in the Boston area.

Andrew (Drew) KRAISINGER grew up in a small town southeast of Pittsburgh, Pennsylvania. His BA in Foreign Affairs at the University of Virginia included study abroad at the National University of Singapore, during which he traveled elsewhere in Southeast Asia. After a few years working in information systems, Drew enrolled in the U-M MBA/MA in Asian Studies program, where he studied Indonesian language and went on summer internships to Poland and Indonesia. Drew then went to work for General Motors in strategic planning, product development, and marketing in Asia-Pacific, Europe, and North America from 1994–2009. After a stint in strategy and product development for the AARP, Drew joined Medecision as Vice-President for Market Strategy, focused on bringing market insights to drive person-centered innovation in the healthcare management industry. He lives in Washington, DC, with his Singaporean wife, Phyllisis, whom he met at NUS and who obtained her PhD in Sociology from U-M, and their two daughters.

Nathaniel (Nat) SIDDALL grew up in Manhattan, Kansas, and obtained his BA in Economics from Brown University and his MBA/MA in Asian Studies from U-M, where he studied Indonesian language. A mountaineering enthusiast, Nat later took to windsurfing and served as Executive Director of the U.S. Windsurfing Association, working from his home in Chelsea, Michigan. He has worked as a journalist and is currently manager of a nature preserve in southwest Michigan. He also enjoys backcountry skiing and gardening.

Richard J. SMITH grew up in Michigan and graduated from the College of Wooster with a BA in Economics and from U-M with the MBA/MA in Asian Studies (1988), during which he founded Suit Yourself, providing Hong Kong tailor-made suits to business students. Rick studied Thai language and moved to Bangkok, Thailand, where he founded and for 21 years managed Innovant Capital, an international business consulting firm providing corporate and financial advisory services to multinationals, Thai corporations, and financial institutions. Rick now heads corporate finance for Tractus Asia, working on M&A, joint-ventures, fund-raising, and pre-IPO preparation and planning for clients in China, India, and Southeast Asia. He lives in Bangkok with his wife and two children.

Michael WACHTEL grew up in New Orleans and obtained a BA in History from the University of Richmond before going to Thailand as a volunteer in camps for Cambodian refugees. He did an MA in Southeast Asian Studies (1996) at U-M, studying Vietnamese language, then moved to the MBA program (1998), during which he did internships in Hanoi with Ford Motor and in Ho Chi Minh City with Mike Dunne's Automotive Resources Asia. Michael worked in foreign exchange sales at Citibank in New York for eight years, after which Citi posted him to Singapore, where he specialized in trading Asian currencies, moving after a few years to Deutsche Bank's Singapore office. During his 10 years in Singapore, Michael continued studying Mandarin Chinese privately while indulging his passions for travel, photography, playing in a rock band, and cooking Chinese cuisine, including once on a TV show while speaking Mandarin. In 2015, Michael moved to Shanghai as Head of China

Institutional Sales for Deutsche, followed later by his wife, Lynn, and their two daughters.

Katherine (Kate) WILSON graduated from the College of William and Mary with a BA in International Relations (1991) and worked as Director for Indonesia Affairs at the US-ASEAN Business Council in Washington, DC, before enrolling in the U-M MBA/MA in Asian Studies program (1999), for which she studied Indonesian language and wrote her thesis on e-commerce in ASEAN! Kate subsequently worked for a series of tech companies including Xbox and Microsoft before becoming Director of Digital Health Solutions for PATH, an international non-profit, which saw her back in Indonesia working with the Ministry of Health to roll out the information system for their national health program. In 2016, Kate became CEO of the Digital Impact Alliance (DIAL) at the United Nations Foundation. She lives in Seattle with her husband and twin sons.

Jay YOSHIOKA was born and grew up in Hawaii. After obtaining his BA in Asian Studies from Pitzer College

(Claremont, California), which included a year's study at Waseda University in Tokyo, he taught English for several years in Japan before moving to Thailand where he studied Thai. Jay then did his MBA/MA in Asian Studies degree at U-M, furthering his study of Thai and Southeast Asia, after which he worked in the travel industry at Northwest Airlines (now Delta) in Minneapolis-St. Paul, then at Cendant RCI in Parsipanny, New Jersey. Since 2002, Jay has worked in consumer lending at Wells Fargo Bank in San Francisco. His passions are travel, which is his biggest activity, particularly to Japan and Thailand, followed by volunteering and supporting grassroots causes such as the Baan Dada Children's Home on the Thai-Myanmar border.

MBA/MA IN ASIAN STUDIES (CENTER FOR SOUTH ASIAN STUDIES)

Jyothi NAMBIAR DAS grew up in Massachusetts with parents who had immigrated to the United States from Kerala, India. She graduated from Swarthmore College with a BA in English Literature and Economics and completed the MBA/MA in Asian Studies at U-M (1997), where she studied Hindi. After graduation she worked in brand management for Unilever, marketing personal care products, then moved to the Bay Area with her husband, a Bengali who grew up in India. She worked at Mattel Interactive/The Learning Company at the height of the Pokemon craze and enjoyed working with colleagues in Japan. Later she worked for LeapFrog on educational toys, then joined LexisNexis in San Francisco, where as Director of Marketing and

Director of Customer Discovery and Innovation, she launched a pilot program in India for a Windows8 legal application. In 2013, Jyothi became Brand Director for schools for Revolution Foods, then took a break from the corporate world to manage construction of her home. She visits India frequently with her husband, Jai Das, and two sons.

CHAPTER 6.

PHOTOS OF GRADUATES AND FACULTY

ASIA BUSINESS CONFERENCES

Asia Business Conference, 2010, reunion, Ann Arbor Front L-R: Scott Labadie, Keith Lublin, Ali Zamiri, Amy Rubin, Jeff Guyton, Bob Wilson Back L-R: Pat Friel, Mike Dunne, Andrew Masterman, Dave Quigley, Ashley McCorkle, Leroy Howard

Asia Business Conference, 2010, reunion dinner at Linda's
L-R: Ashley McCorkle, Brad Farnsworth, Pat Friel, Leroy Howard, Jay Yoshioka, Jeff Guyton

Asia Business Conference, 2010, reunion dinner at Linda's
L-R: Bob Wilson, Ali Zamiri, Andrew Masterman

Asia Business Conference, 2012, Ann Arbor
L-R: Joe Osha, Simon Kahn, Linda Lim, Rick Smith, A. Rama Krishna

25th Asia Business Conference, 2015, Ann Arbor
L-R: Mike Wachtel, LeAnn Eriksson, Pete Gosling, Andrew Masterman, Joe Osha, Bob Wilson, Linda Lim

Asia Business Conference, 2015, dinner at Linda's
L-R: LeAnn Eriksson, Martha Masterman Gordon, Andrew Masterman

Alumni speakers with Linda Lim and Arif Iqball, Asia Business Conference, 2017

GRADUATES' PHOTOS

Mike Dunne, Linda Lim, and Rick Smith, Bangkok, 1994

Mike Wachtel, Steve Dean, and Linda Lim,
Singapore, 2006

Linda Lim, Rick Smith, Mark Guthrie, and
Brendan Kavaney, Bangkok, 2007

Mike Wachtel, Gunter Dufey, Linda Lim, and
Simon Kahn with other MBA alumni, Singapore,
2009

Chinese New Year, San Francisco, 2011 L-R: Amy Rubin, Brendan Kavaney, Pat Friel, Paul Ziots, Jay Yoshioka, Pepper Kavaney

Ali Zamiri and Andrew Masterman, Orcas Island, Washington, 2011

Gunter Dufey, Mike Dunne, Linda Lim, and Pete Gosling at Mike's book launch, November, 2011

L-R: Mike Wachtel, Simon Kahn, Linda Lim, and Mike Dunne, Singapore, 2012

L-R: Ben Simar, Mike Little, Linda Lim, Tom Stanley, and Pat Cranley, Shanghai, 2013

Mike Dunne guest lectures to MBAs in 2013

Drew Kraisinger, Linda Lim, and Paul Churchill,
Ann Arbor, ca. 1992

Drew Kraisinger and Paul Churchill,
Washington, DC, 2014

Tom Stanley guest lectures to MBAs in 2015

Gunter Dufey in 1987

Pete Gosling

*Ken and Jane Lieberthal with Pat
Cranley, Shanghai, 2017*

David Methe

Vladimir Pucik

Tom Roehl

Clyde Stoltenberg

Vern Terpstra

Heidi Tietjen

David Weinstein

Ena Schlorff

CHAPTER 7.

U-M'S ASIAN STUDIES CENTERS

U-M'S ASIAN STUDIES CENTERS

CJS—The Center for Japanese Studies

The University of Michigan Center for Japanese Studies (CJS) promotes and disseminates research on Japan, fosters communication among diverse disciplines, and encourages new approaches in the understanding of Japan and its place in the world. CJS serves as a home to graduate students, faculty from a variety of disciplines and professional schools, visiting artists and scholars, and community organizations pursuing Japan-related interests and activities at the University of Michigan. Founded in 1947, CJS is the oldest interdisciplinary center in the United States devoted exclusively to Japanese Studies. CJS is also part of U-M's East Asia U.S. Department of Education Title VI National Resource Center.

CSAS—The Center for South Asian Studies

The Center for South Asian Studies (CSAS) at the University of Michigan is a national leader in promoting a deeper understanding of India, Pakistan, Afghanistan, Nepal, Bangladesh, Bhutan, and Sri Lanka. The center offers a range of area-related courses taught by outstanding faculty, a scholarly lecture series, conferences, study abroad fellowships, student colloquiums, and opportunities to volunteer, sponsor, and cosponsor a variety of events. CSAS is also a U.S. Department of Education designated National Resource Center, funded to develop area studies education for this region of the world.

CSEAS—The Center for Southeast Asian Studies

The Center for Southeast Asian Studies (CSEAS), one of the oldest centers in the United States devoted to the SEA region, was founded in 1961 and has been a National Resource Center with FLAS awards since 1964. The center is committed to promoting a broader and deeper understanding of Southeast Asia and its histories, cultures, and peoples by providing resources for faculty, students, and the community to learn and disseminate knowledge about the region. We have graduated more than 230 MAs in SEAS and 450 PhD students in the past 50 years, many of whom have gone on to leadership roles in academia, government, business, and non-profits. CSEAS administers an MA degree in SEAS, an MBA/MA, a dual degree MA in SEAS/Public Policy, and a Graduate Certificate in SEAS available to PhD and professional MA students. Some 50 non-language SEA area courses are offered in 10 disciplines and 6 professional schools. CSEAS supports faculty, students, and staff throughout the university; brings SEA scholars and performers to campus; and engages in extensive programming that includes lectures, arts events, conferences, and outreach.

LRCCS—The Lieberthal-Rogel Center for Chinese Studies

The Kenneth G. Lieberthal and Richard H. Rogel Center for Chinese Studies (LRCCS) is the premier place on the University of Michigan campus to gain access to resources on China, including leading scholars, ongoing projects, and funding for faculty and student research. It houses experts in nearly every major facet of Chinese studies, ranging from literature and history to law and public health. Chinese studies at the University of Michigan formally began in 1930 with the establishment of an Oriental Civilizations Program. In 1961, the Center for Chinese Studies (CCS) was established. In 2014 the center's name was changed in recognition of a generous gift from U-M alumni Richard Rogel and the contributions of professor emeritus Kenneth Lieberthal. It has become one of the nation's most prominent centers devoted to a deeper understanding of China, past and present. LRCCS is part of U-M's East Asia National Resource Center, a prestigious designation awarded by the U.S. Department of Education.

CHAPTER 8.

DIRECTORY OF GRADUATES

UNIVERSITY OF MICHIGAN MBA/MA ASIAN STUDIES ALUMNI

*Counted twice (CCS and CSEAS)

MBA/MA CCS (23)

1982 Eric Zwisler ezwisler@gmail.com Shanghai, China

1988 Jeffrey Bistrong jbistrong@gmail.com Boston, MA

1988 Wm Patrick Cranley wmpatrick.cranley@asiamedia.net Shanghai, China

1988 Paul Lowrey plowrey@pacbell.net San Francisco, CA

1989 Peter M. Christian petermchristian6@gmail.com Houston, TX

1989 Charles Dever Todd, no contact info

1990 Michael J. Dunne (also CSEAS) Michael.dunne@dunneautomotive.com, yougotthemike@gmail.com Hong Kong and San Diego, CA*

1992 Amy Rubin Friel (also CSEAS) amyfriel827@gmail.com San Jose, CA*

1993 MBA, BA ALC Thomas Stanley Thomas.stanley@kpmg.com Shanghai, China

1993 Wesley Sealand nsealand@gmail.com Portland, OR

1994 Michael F. Little, Jr mlittlejr@hotmail.com, mlittl48@ford.com Bangkok, Thailand

1994 Nancy Yu Kochansky nancyyu0808@gmail.com Bronxville, NY

1995 Thomas Rosenthal tmr1776@gmail.com San Diego, CA

1997 Joan Stephenson jlstephjl@gmail.com New York, NY

1997 Thomas M. Horn Thomas.m.horn@gmail.com Hong Kong

1997 Simon Kahn simonkahn@google.com Singapore

1999 Frank Chong fchong@umich.edu Los Angeles, CA

1999 Alexandra Conroy 8ailian8@gmail.com Chicago, IL

2001 Joel Samuels joelsamuels15@hotmail.com Davis, CA

2002 Jason Conway jasonconway1@gmail.com Hartford, CT

2004 Benjamin Simar bensimar@gmail.com Hong Kong

2003 MA, 2010 MBA Scott Labadie labadie3@gmail.com Seattle, WA

MBA/MA CJS (33)

1983 David Quigley dave@thsinternational.com Carmel, IN

1987 Avula Rama Krishna krishna.arama@gmail.com Greenwich, CT

1987 James Lannen, jlannen@umich.edu, Ann Arbor, MI

1988 Paul C. Schomburg pschomburg@yahoo.com, pschomburg@us.panasonic.com Washington, DC

1988 Nancy Ann Nettleton, no contact info

1989 Adam Orlan, aorlan2@gmail.com Richmond, VA

1989 Jeffrey S. Protzel Jeffrey.protzel@gmail.com Slidell, LA

1989 James C. Roche eph85@msn.com Glenview, IL

1990 Paul Martin pit2210@gmail.com Menlo Park, CA

1990 Michelle Lynn Gross, no contact info

1991 Jeffrey H. Guyton jguyton@mazdaeur.com Leverkusen, Germany

1991 Tara LeAnn Eriksson tara@spaceforgrace.com Cologne, Germany

1991 Leroy Howard ljhoakland@comcast.net Oakland, CA

1991 David G. Whetstone dave.whetstone@gmail.com San Francisco, CA

1991 Ali J. Zamiri azamiri@gmail.com San Diego, CA

1992 David Most mostd45@yahoo.com New Jersey

1992 Joseph A. Osha samurai700@hotmail.com Oakland, CA

1993 Bruce W. Irish bwirish@gmail.com Newbury Park, CA

1993 Andrew Masterman avm@umich.edu Philadelphia, PA

1993 Ashley McCorkle Ashley.mccorkle@gmail.com Oakland, CA

1993 Cynthia Tragge-Lakra ctraggelakra@gmail.com

1994 Paul M. Ziots paul.ziots@gmail.com Foster City, CA

1995 Arif Iqball aiqball@me.com Tokyo, Japan

1995 Keith A. Lublin klublin@hotmail.com West Bloomfield, MI

1996 Christopher Derose derose@umich.edu Ann Arbor, MI

1997 Brendan C. Buescher Brendan_buescher@mckinsey.com

1997 Donald A. Semones dsemones@mac.com Ann Arbor, MI

1998 Daniel Heilbrunn dheilbru@gmail.com Vancouver, Canada

1998 Robert G. Wilson robertgwilsonjr@yahoo.com Cleveland, OH

2001 Aundrea Almond aunj01@yahoo.com Wilmington, DE

2003 Scot Kojola skojola@umich.edu High Point, NC

2005 Neil Harrison neiladamharrison@gmail.com New York, NY

2008 Simone Heron simoneheron@gmail.com New York, NY

MBA/MA CSEAS (19)

1986 Nathan Johnson nsjohnson@lt-indonesia.com Jakarta, Indonesia

1986 Audrey King Audrey.king17@gmail.com Arlington, VA

1987 Steven Don Dean steve.dean@refinitiv.com Jakarta, Indonesia

1988 Richard J. Smith Richard.smith@tractus-asia.com Bangkok, Thailand

1990 Michael J. Dunne (also CCS)

Michael.dunne@zozogo.com, yougotthemike@gmail.com San Diego, CA*

1991 Patrick Friel pcfriel@tutanota.com San Jose, CA

1992 Amy Rubin Friel (also CCS) amyfriel827@gmail.com San Jose, CA*

1994 Paul Churchill pr_churchill@hotmail.com Munich, Germany

1994 Jay Yoshioka flyintl@yahoo.com San Francisco, CA

1994 Michael Helmus, no contact info

1995 Andrew Kraisinger ready4growth@gmail.com Washington, DC

1996, 1998 Michael Wachtel wachatelly@gmail.com, michael.wachtel@db.com Shanghai, China

1997 Nathaniel Siddall nathanielsatsouthlake@yahoo.com Chelsea, MI

1998 Patrick J. Griffin patrick.griffin@escaladeinc.com Evansville, IN

1999 Martha Masterman Gordon martha.l.gordon@gmail.com Ann Arbor, MI

1999 Katherine Wilson wilsonkh30@hotmail.com Seattle, WA

2002 Jon Blumenauer jon.blumenauer@hutani.com Portland, OR

2002 Mark Guthrie mguthrie@umich.edu; mguthrie@runbox.com Bangkok, Thailand

2007 Brendan Kavaney bkavaney@gmail.com San Francisco, CA

MBA/MA CSAS (1)

1997 Jyothi Nambiar Das jyothidas3@gmail.com Menlo Park, CA